INHERIT THE WIND BY JEROME LAWRENCE AND ROBERT E. LEE

Intelligent Education

INFLUENCE PUBLISHERS

Nashville, Tennessee

BRIGHT NOTES: Inherit the Wind

www.BrightNotes.com

No part of this publication may be used or reproduced in any manner whatsoever without written permission, except in the case of brief quotations in critical articles and reviews. For permissions, contact Influence Publishers http://www.influencepublishers.com.

ISBN: 978-1-645423-04-1 (Paperback)
ISBN: 978-1-645423-05-8 (eBook)

Published in accordance with the U.S. Copyright Office Orphan Works and Mass Digitization report of the register of copyrights, June 2015.

Originally published by Monarch Press.
Bruce E. Johnson, 1979
2020 Edition published by Influence Publishers.

Interior design by Lapiz Digital Services. Cover Design by Thinkpen Designs.

Printed in the United States of America.

Library of Congress Cataloging-in-Publication Data forthcoming.
Names: Intelligent Education
Title: BRIGHT NOTES: Inherit the Wind
Subject: STU004000 STUDY AIDS / Book Notes

CONTENTS

INTRODUCTION TO LAWRENCE AND LEE

The most cherished freedom preserved for the American people in the original Bill of Rights is the freedom of speech. Yet at times throughout our country's history, certain groups and individuals, through either covert methods or state and federal legislation, have sought to restrict our fundamental right to think and to communicate our thoughts to others. As the United States attempted to recover from the effects of World War II and entered the decade of the Korean and Cold Wars, two young playwrights, alarmed by the attempts of a Republican senator from Wisconsin to persecute and victimize individuals whose only "crime" was to exercise their right to think, wrote a play to protest the restrictions upon the right to freedom of speech.

Jerome Lawrence and Robert E. Lee turned their attentions and talents to an earlier era in American history when, once before, an individual's right to think and to speak had been jeopardized: the Scopes Monkey Trial in Dayton, Tennessee, in July of 1925. A high school biology teacher by the name of John Scopes had challenged a recently passed state law that prohibited teachers from discussing the theory of evolution with their students. The Scopes Trial in the twenties and the McCarthy hearings in the fifties both focused the country's attention on the conflict between the individual's freedom of speech and governmental control.

John Thomas Scopes eventually went free, Senator Joseph McCarthy was later censured by his colleagues, and "the evolution law" was finally repealed, but Jerome Lawrence and Robert E. Lee have created a drama that transcends each of these individual events. Translated into over thirty languages, *Inherit the Wind* has emerged as a modern theatrical classic that continues to defend, long after the repeal of a law or the death of a leader, the individual's right to think and the freedom to express his thoughts.

ROBERT E. LEE AND JEROME LAWRENCE

Robert E. Lee. Robert E. Lee, playwright, director, and producer, was born on October 15, 1918, in the Ohio community of Elyria. When he was seventeen, he began Ohio Wesleyan University, attracted primarily by the Perkins Observatory telescope, which at that time was the fourth largest in the world. Lee worked extensively with the Perkins telescope, but also became interested in radio broadcasting. While at Ohio Wesleyan he worked as a radio announcer for two stations in Columbus and wrote for another in Cincinnati. As his infatuation for radio drama spread to include campus theatre, Lee's grades and his dreams of becoming an astronomer began to feel the effects. "I was going through a discovery of the excitement of communication," Lee has remarked about his experience at Ohio Wesleyan. "I decided that an astronomer was essentially an observer, a receptor; I wanted to be a source of emanations, a communicator."

Two years later, at the age of nineteen, Lee moved north to Cleveland where he worked as a radio announcer and writer. In the following year, 1938, he settled in New York, where he worked for the radio advertising firm of Young and Rubicam as a director and producer. By January of 1940, Lee was shuttling back and forth between New York and Hollywood as an assistant producer for various radio shows.

Jerome Lawrence. Jerome Lawrence was born in Cleveland, Ohio, on July 14, 1915. At the age of eighteen, Jerome Lawrence enrolled in Ohio State University "to be a newspaperman;" he recalls, "but always a playwright, or somehow associated with the theatre," and his experience there hastened Lawrence toward his goal. During the school year he performed in numerous campus theatrical productions. Each summer after he began attending Ohio State, he wrote and directed plays and musical comedies for summer theatres in Pennsylvania and Massachusetts.

A few months after his graduation, Lawrence returned to Ohio where he began work first as a reporter and telegraph editor for the Wilmington News-Journal and then as editor of the New Lexington Daily News. Lawrence moved to California in December of 1937 where he worked as continuity editor and writer-director-producer for a Beverly Hills radio station until 1939, when he was hired by Columbia Broadcasting Service as a senior staff writer. Although Lawrence worked for CBS radio for the next three years (1939-1941), he never abandoned his goal of becoming a "working playwright."

Lawrence And Lee In Collaboration. Although Jerome Lawrence and Robert E. Lee were born only three years apart in cities separated by less than thirty miles, attended neighboring universities the same year, were both aspiring playwrights, and had simultaneously worked in radio stations in Ohio and California, the two had never met. Each had heard of the other, but until early 1942 their paths had never crossed.

"Actors would say that we should meet," Lawrence recollects, "and then in early 1942 we finally did meet: downstairs of CBS at Colbee's restaurant on January 23, 1942."

"I had come back [to New York] to work on the revived *March of Time*," Lee recalls. "Jer was doing a CBS war series, *They Live Forever*. We both knew of each other's work, were amazed that our lives had been so parallel, [and] decided to try doing some freelance writing together."

That winter they collaborated on several radio shows, and in one week alone six of their collaborations were broadcast on the nation's airwaves. Variety ran this headline: Lawrence And Lee Take Over Radio.

In 1946, four years after they had met and first collaborated, Jerome Lawrence and Robert Lee legally and formally organized the partnership since known as Lawrence and Lee. During the next four years the radio "Whiz Kids" were acclaimed popular and critical successes with such programs as *Hallmark Playhouse*, *Halls of Ivy*, *Favorite Story*, and *The Railroad Hour*.

On January 29, 1948; though, their musical *Look, Ma, I'm Dancin'* opened at the Adelphi Theatre in New York City under the direction of George Abbott and Jerome Robbins and starring Nancy Walker. This marked the first meeting of the team of Lawrence and Lee with Broadway, and enabled the playwrights to gain valuable experience working with the professional people associated with a Broadway production. Lawrence describes it as a "fine first experience in the Broadway theatre" and "a moderate success; what we always called a 'nervous hit.'"

The limited financial success of *Look, Ma, I'm Dancin'* did not enable Lawrence and Lee to devote their talents full time to stage drama, but it supplied the necessary encouragement for them to continue writing plays as they supported themselves with hundreds of radio and television programs. It was to be six years, however, before they would return to Broadway with the next Lawrence and Lee production.

Inherit The Wind. Alarmed by the wave of McCarthyism that had begun to sweep the country, the team of Lawrence and Lee began work in the early 1950s on what was to become their most notable success, *Inherit the Wind.* Lawrence and Lee chose as the genesis of the play the Scopes Monkey Trial of 1925, wherein a young biology teacher had been tried and convicted of teaching the theory of evolution to his students. The spirit and message of the play transcends time, though, and its **theme** "the right to think" applied to the McCarthy era as well as to the turbulent sixties and seventies. Lawrence and Lee spent nearly a year researching, drafting, and rewriting the play, yet every major producer on Broadway turned it down. Only a chance meeting with a friend of Margo Jones, founder and director of the Dallas Theatre-in-the-Round, led to the eventual premiere of *Inherit the Wind* in Dallas in January of 1955.

After three successful weeks in Dallas before sell-out crowds, the Broadway director - producer Herman Shumlin took the play to New York where it opened with Paul Muni, Ed Begly, and Tony Randall at the National Theatre on April 21, 1955, and ran for an astounding 806 performances and received five Tony awards, the Donaldson award, the Variety Critics award, the Outer-Circle Critics award, and the British Drama Critics award. The play, now considered a modern classic and translated into thirty-one languages, established Lawrence and Lee within the ranks of prominent American playwrights and took from radio two of its brightest and most gifted writers.

After the wonderful success of *Inherit the Wind*, Lawrence and Lee collaborated on a host of plays, some more successful than others. These included *Auntie Mame*, which dramatizes Patrick Dennis' sprawling novel of the same name, and *The Night Thoreau Spent in Jail*. Just as *Inherit the Wind* uses the Scopes trial as a parable for the McCarthy era, *The Night Thoreau Spent in Jail* depicts an actual event in Thoreau's life as a parable for the protest against the Vietnamese War. In the play, Thoreau demonstrates his philosophy of peaceful civil disobedience when he is imprisoned for refusing to pay taxes which he felt were being used to support the Mexican War. Lawrence and Lee chose Ohio State University as the site for the world premiere of *The Night Thoreau Spent in Jail*, proving that "theatre does not have to stem from New York."

Lawrence and Lee live within miles of one another in California and still collaborate. They feel that *Inherit the Wind* and *The Night Thoreau Spent in Jail* are their two best works thus far; when asked to comment on their work and their position in American theatre they replied: "Critics try to cubby-hole us, as they do Neil Simon and Tennessee Williams. But we sometimes confuse people because we try to make our comedy serious and our serious plays funny.... To disagree - to dissent without violence - is to comment on the human condition."

The final judgment on Lawrence and Lee and their work has not yet been made, but their manuscripts and memoranda are preserved in the New York Public Library to await later assessment. Few other playwrights of this troubled century have written so dramatically and prolifically about the issues of their own day, and it may require a passage of time before the total value of their literary work can be measured.

THE WORKS OF LAWRENCE AND LEE

Plays

Look, Ma, I'm Dancin' (musical), Adelphi Theatre, New York City, January 29, 1948.

Inherit the Wind, National Theatre, New York City, April 21, 1955 (Random House, 1955).

Shangri-La (musical, with James Hilton), Winter Garden Theatre, New York City, June 13, 1956.

Auntie Mame (suggested by book Auntie Mame by Patrick Dennis), Broadhurst Theatre, New York City, October 31, 1956 (Vanguard Press, 1957).

The Gang's All Here, Ambassador Theatre, New York City, October 1, 1959 (World Publishing Company, 1960).

Only in America, Cort Theatre, New York City, November, 1959 (Samuel French, 1960).

A Call on Kurpin, Broadhurst Theatre, New York City, May 25, 1961 (Samuel French, 1961).

The Diamond Orchard, Henry Miller Theatre, New York City, February 10, 1965.

Live Spelled Backwards (Jerome Lawrence), Beverly Hills Playhouse, January 14, 1966 (Dramatists Play Service, 1970).

Mame (musical, with Jerry Herman), Winter Garden Theatre, New York City, May 24, 1966 (Random House, 1967).

Sparks Fly Upward, McFarlin Auditorium, Dallas, Texas, December 3, 1967 (Dramatists Play Service, 1969).

Dear World (musical, with Jerry Herman), Mark Hellinger Theatre, New York City, February 6, 1969.

The Incomparable Max, Barter Theatre, Virginia, June 24, 1969; Royale Theatre, New York City, October 19, 1971 (Hill and Wang, 1972).

The Crocodile Smile, State Theatre of North Carolina, Flatrock, August, 1970 (Dramatists Play Service, 1972).

The Night Thoreau Spent in Jail, Ohio State University, April 21, 1970 (Hill and Wang, 1970).

Jabberwock, Ohio State University, November 18, 1972 (Samuel French, 1974).

Ten Days That Shook the World (Robert E. Lee), *Freud Playhouse, UCLA, May 31, 1973.*

First Monday in October, Cleveland Play House, October, 1975.

Books

Lawrence, Jerome. *Actor: The Life and Times of Paul Muni.* New York: G.P. Putnam's Sons, 1974.

___. *Off Mike.* New York: Duel, Sloan, and Pierce, 1944.

___. *Oscar the Ostrich.* New York: Random House, 1940. Lee, Robert E. Television: *The Revolutionary Industry.* New York: Duel, Sloan, and Pierce, 1944.

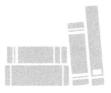

INHERIT THE WIND

THE TITLE

He that troubleth his own house shall inherit the wind, and the fool shall be servant to the wise in heart.

Prov. 11:29

Playwrights Jerome Lawrence and Robert E. Lee wrote *Inherit the Wind* knowing from the very beginning exactly what the title of the play was to be. Lee had discovered the passage in Proverbs which prefaces their drama and which supplied them with not only a title for *Inherit the Wind*, but which also helped convey one of the most important **themes** in the play. The title and the quotation from Proverbs warn the theatre audience that it is possible, through overzealousness, "to destroy that which you hope to save."

The passage from Proverbs first appears at the close of the prayer meeting, when Brady assumes control of the townspeople from the Reverend Brown. The avid Fundamentalist's overwhelming desire to defeat and destroy Bert Cates and the forces of evolution leads him to an emotional and irrational act - the calling of the Lord to strike down not only Cates, but his daughter Rachel as well. But his fervor, instead, causes him to lose, to destroy that which he had hoped to save: his daughter, his followers, and, in a sense, the respect and dignity of the Fundamentalist faith.

Ironically, Brady's quotation is resurrected by his foremost critic, Hornbeck, who cites it as the Great Commoner's **epitaph**. Brady's overzealousness occurs at various levels: his desire to prosecute Cates spawns worldwide attention on the trial and, thus, on the theory of evolution; his desire to defeat Drummond and the defenders of evolution overcomes his sense of reason, and leads him to the witness stand; his desire to defend a strict Fundamentalist interpretation of the Bible provokes inadequate and ridiculous replies to Drummond's questions; and, finally, his desire to recover his lost dignity and respect on the final day of the trial evokes his final rejection and, indirectly, his death. Brady's overzealousness destroyed his victory over Drummond and the evolutionists, his dignity and reputation as a Fundamentalist leader, and the strength of the Fundamentalist religion.

Matthew Harrison Brady, the Reverend Jeremiah Brown, and the other avid Fundamentalists each had "the right to think…the right to be wrong," but their lack of control, their lack of reason in the face of extreme emotionalism led them, as it did Joseph McCarthy, "to be overzealous, to destroy that which [they] hoped to save - so that nothing is left but emptiness." Lawrence and Lee's message, their warning, still holds true today - and will, as well, tomorrow.

THEMES

The search for **themes** in literary and other artistic works can often become an overzealous quest on the part of instructors and students alike. Without due caution, without some perspective on the role of **theme** in a work, the search can obliterate more than it uncovers. Two or three-sentence summaries do not do justice to a fine piece of literature; when reduced to such, outstanding works oftentimes are reduced in the eyes of the students to little more than overblown cliches. **Themes** can aid the student in sorting out ideas, but "they themselves," as Robert Longsworth emphasized in *The Design of Drama*, "are not the essence of the work." For the teacher who values **theme** above all else, above all other aspects of a play and their total impact and effect on the theatre audience, the quotation that serves as the source of the title of *Inherit the Wind* should be carefully considered.

The following list and discussion of major **themes** present in *Inherit the Wind* does not attempt to capsulize all that Jerome Lawrence and Robert E. Lee comment on or suggest in their play; analysis of **theme**, like that of structure and character, retains its value only when viewed in the proper perspective - as one part of an entire work and total effect. That final effect cannot be summarized in two or three sentences without damaging the authors' work; it comes only from additional viewing and/or reading of the play.

Right To Think. Basic to the action of the play is the conflict over the individual's right to think, or, as Henry Drummond says, "the right to be wrong." Although we know that the thought-control tactics of McCarthyism helped inspire Lawrence and Lee to turn their attention to yet another time in American history when the freedoms of thought and speech were threatened, the conflict between thought-control and enlightenment, or between the individual conscience and the laws of the state, is never limited by either time or geographic boundaries. Nor is it a privilege granted either to just minorities or to just majorities, for, as Drummond illustrates at the close of *Inherit the Wind*, Matthew Harrison Brady has the same right that Bert Cates, Rachel Brown, or E. K. Hornbeck has: the right to think and the freedom to express those thoughts to others.

Conformity. Although freedom of speech is often guaranteed and protected in the democratic principles of a government, many persons deny themselves this right and others, for they are the victims of conformity. A few individuals, like Bert Cates and Henry Drummond, are unafraid to speak out, regardless of the consequences, but most people find themselves in situations similar to Rachel Brown's - the fear of what "others" will think, say, or do prevents them from voicing opinions that may be different from the standards set by society. Henry Drummond emphasizes a belief held by Jerome Lawrence, Robert E. Lee, and Clarence Darrow, as well - it only takes one person to stand up for what he or she believes is right, and even though he or she will probably stand alone, at least at first, he or she will make it easier for the next individualist to speak out.

Science And Religion. Running parallel to the conflict between the individual conscience and the laws of the state is that between the theory of evolution and the Fundamentalist belief in a literal interpretation of the Bible in *Inherit the Wind*. Bert Cates and Henry Drummond both attempt to convince the townspeople of Hillsboro that the theory of evolution and the Biblical story of creation can coexist in the minds of men if only they will relax their grasp on the idea that each of the first six days was precisely twenty-four hours long - an idea that Drummond effectively shatters in court when he points out that the sun was not created until the fourth day. Darwin's theory of evolution did not attempt to explain the origin of life; instead, the English scientist began with the assumption that life had somehow been created and tried to show how individuals, plant and animal, grew and developed into their present forms over a time period spanning millions of years. Thus it appears that if one would restrain himself or herself from limiting each of the first Biblical "days" to twenty-four hours, he or she could reconcile both the *Origin of Species* and the Bible in his or her mind.

Progress. Both thought-control and conformity impede progress, and Lawrence and Lee use Matthew Harrison Brady to epitomize and illustrate this belief. Just as it is Brady who wishes to ban evolution from the classrooms and who expects the members of the jury to conform to society's standards, it is Matthew Harrison Brady who inhibits progress, symbolizes the past, and is deserted in the end by his followers who have journeyed forward. Yet, as Drummond warns, progress carries with it a price: loss of privacy, increased responsibilities, polluted skies and streams, and a departure from faith in outdated traditions.

Right And Truth. In the context of the play, Drummond defines Right as being determined by society, while Truth, which remains ever-constant and ever-elusive, serves as a direction for man to follow. The conflict arises, then, when, as in the case of Bert Cates, the search for Truth veers from the path of Right. At that point the individual must choose between his conscience and conformity, and must be prepared to live with his decision.

Trial Of The Townspeople. While the Hillsboro jury sits in judgment of Bert Cates, the theatre audience of *Inherit the Wind* sits in judgment of the townspeople themselves. The townspeople, in fact, are more visible throughout the play than Cates; from the preparations for Brady's arrival, the picnic, jury selection, and the prayer meeting to Brady's testimony, the announcement of the verdict, and the collapse of their leader the audience can watch and assess their actions and words.

As the play and the trial begin, the townspeople are clearly Fundamentalist supporters of Brady and are marked by their concern with the financial benefits of the trial. The prayer meeting reveals two aspects of their character: their imitative and emotional approach to religion, and their capacity to reject their leader (in this case the Reverend Brown) if he betrays their expectations. They invest their support entirely in Brady, yet when he is ridiculed by Drummond many of them desert him. They find Cates guilty, yet the minimum fine does not offend them as it does the prosecution. By the end of the trial and the play the townspeople have begun to change, but, as Cates pointed out earlier to Rachel, it is never a choice of black or white, right or wrong. Drummond has not converted them into evolutionists, but he has convinced some of them that evolution is not necessarily an evil categorically to be rejected.

The ending of the play is inclusive as far as the townspeople are concerned, but the playwrights hint strongly at what is in store for them. They have rejected Brown, they have rejected Brady; yet they have not endorsed Drummond either. It remains for them to decide for themselves, as Rachel has done, exactly what they will believe, but Henry Drummond has opened their minds and the first step towards progress and enlightenment has been taken.

To aid students in their study of drama, plays have by tradition been classified into various types, according to their overall structure and total effect. Most common amongst these types are the tragedy, comedy, history, romance, melodrama, and problem play. It is in this latter category, the problem play, that Lawrence and Lee's *Inherit the Wind* falls.

Although in a general sense the term problem play could apply to any drama which deals with a problem of human life, it more specifically refers to the semimodern "drama of ideas," which voices a protest against a social or moral problem existing in society. The problem play combines elements from tragedy, comedy, history, and melodrama. It is often tragic in tone as it presents an often painful human dilemma; generally uses as its framework an event or person in history to act as a spokesman for present times; contains elements of humor and quite often has "happy" endings; and incorporates great emotion. It is generally **didactic** in nature, as it often appeals to the intellect in its attempts to further progress by drawing attention to social evils. Its major flaw is that it sometimes tends to oversimplify situations (one criticism of *Inherit the Wind*), and, for the sake of dramatic intensity, to become overmelodramatic. Examples of outstanding problem plays would include Robert Bolt's *A Man for All Seasons*, George Bernard Shaw's *Saint Joan,* and Lawrence and Lee's *Inherit the Wind*.

Tragedy is represented in *Inherit the Wind* through the reversal of fortune and the death of the tragic figure Matthew Harrison Brady; elements of comedy can be found in the portrayal of the townspeople; from melodrama the playwrights employ strong emotion and the happy ending, wherein the "good" characters are rewarded and the "bad" punished. The structure and subject matter of the play reflect the strong aspect of history in *Inherit the Wind*. Although Lawrence and Lee's work cannot be classified as a pure history play, it still must overcome the double dilemma facing all history related dramas: it must satisfy those audience members who are familiar with the persons and/or events being portrayed on the stage, and it must entertain those in the audience who know nothing about them. Finally, *Inherit the Wind* attacks a dangerous social evil-thought-control - and attempts to teach, lead, and entertain its audience.

THE PLAY AS HISTORY

Inherit the Wind **is not history. The events which took place in Dayton, Tennessee, during the scorching July of 1925 are clearly the genesis of this play. It has, however, an exodus entirely its own.**

After nearly a year of concentrated research on the Scopes Monkey Trial, Jerome Lawrence and Robert E. Lee set aside their books and notes and wrote the drama *Inherit the Wind.* The passage quoted above is taken from the preface they wrote to accompany the work. *Inherit the Wind* was not intended to serve as a documentary of the Scopes trial; its characters have, as Lawrence and Lee point out, "life and language...and names of their own." Yet the fact that the Scopes Trial served as an inspiration for *Inherit the Wind* immediately raises the question of what characters, situations, words, speeches, and actions actually did exist or occur in Dayton, Tennessee, in the year 1925.

To begin with the obvious, the basic conflicts are identical: the teaching of the theory of evolution in the public schools versus legislative control of teachers; the theory of evolution versus a strict, literal interpretation of the Bible; a young science teacher versus the law; and two famous lawyers, one a Fundamentalist, the other an agnostic, versus one another.

Preliminary stage directions set the action only in a "small town" and the time as "summer-not too long ago." Later the small town is called Hillsboro - the fictional Dayton, Tennessee (in the play Chattanooga, Dayton's nearest large city, is mentioned several times). In both the trial and the play the heat seemed unbearable. The majority of the characters of *Inherit the Wind* are purely the products of the playwrights' imaginations, but several of the main characters and a few of the minor ones had as their models personalities actually present at Dayton.

Howard Blair, for instance, a student of Bert Cates and a witness in the play, appears to have been based on Howard Morgan, who also testified to what he had been taught in regards to the theory of evolution. Tom Davenport bears a striking resemblance to Tom Stewart, circuit district attorney and chief legal counsel for the prosecution. The Judge, though a minor figure in the play, seems to share many of the characteristics of the Dayton figure, Judge John T. Raulston, who presided over the Scopes trial.

The center of the controversy, Bertram Cates, is a clear reconstruction of the young, single science teacher who taught at Dayton and was charged with teaching evolution, John T. Scopes. His close friend Rachel Brown (and her father) was totally a creation of Lawrence and Lee's. E. K. Hornbeck is none other than H. L. Mencken, the cynical reporter from the Baltimore Sun (the Baltimore Herald in the play) who ridiculed the townspeople of Dayton and William Jennings Bryan.

The two legal giants in the play, Matthew Harrison Brady and Henry Drummond, had as their models two giants of their day, William Jennings Bryan and Clarence Darrow. The similarities between these two characters and their actual counterparts will emerge as parallels between the play and history are discussed scene by scene.

Act One, Scene One. The playwrights' description of Hillsboro is an accurate reflection of Dayton, Tennessee, in 1925. Although an actual year is never mentioned in the play, references are never made to any persons, events, or inventions which occurred after 1925. The month, though, of July, and the terrible heat are historically accurate. Howard Blair, as mentioned before, resembles fourteen-year-old Howard Morgan of Dayton, although Melinda appears to be entirely fictitious. One of Howard's lines - "Your old man's a monkey" - was a popular phrase in Dayton during the trial.

The character of Rachel Brown and her relationship with Bert Cates was added by the playwrights to increase dramatic tension and to create a subplot to help sustain audience interest. In a similar manner, Cates is shown in jail; John T Scopes, however, never spent a single day or night in jail for his "crime." Cates and Scopes, in addition to age, personality, and outward appearance, also taught the same biology book, Hunter's *Civic Biology*, to their science classes.

Preparations by the people of Hillsboro for the trial and the arrival of Matthew Harrison Brady are accurate reconstructions of the welcome given William Jennings Bryan when he arrived in Dayton a few days before the trial began. In both cases, the financial interests of the people were obvious. The banner "Read Your Bible" actually hung on the outside wall of the Rhea County Courthouse in Dayton. The hawkers, Bible salesmen, and monkeys were all a part of Dayton's "county fair." Although H.L. Mencken's conversations with the people of Dayton were never recorded, the spirit with which he descended upon them is reflected through E. K. Hornbeck in *Inherit the Wind*, as are some of his phrases, including the famous term "the Bible Belt."

The description of Matthew Harrison Brady - three-time candidate for the presidency, Chautauqua speaker, famous orator, balding, paunchy, and sixty-five years old-is an accurate description of William Jennings Bryan as he alighted from the train in Dayton - including his aversion to the heat, his dislike for the "big cities of the North" (brought about primarily by urban reporters like Mencken who were not swayed by his appeal to the common man), his role as a leader in the suffrage movement, advisor to President Wilson, and defender of the faith. Bryan, also, was infatuated by food; it was reported that while in Dayton he would carry a bunch of radishes with him to eat, and would occasionally bring fresh vegetables into a restaurant to be prepared along with his meal.

In a similar manner, the description of Henry Drummond in the first scene matches Clarence Darrow - agnostic, cunning, defender of murderers, Chicago lawyer, slouching man, who always maintained that society had to share the blame for the crimes of any lawbreaker.

Act One, Scene Two. In the play the trial proceedings take place in the courtyard in order to permit all of the spectators to view the action. In Dayton, Judge Raulston moved the trial outdoors once in eight days in order to relieve the stress on the courthouse floor and to seek relief from the heat. The jury selection scene reflects two facts from Dayton: the townspeople believed that the jurors would have the best seats and thus were anxious to be selected, and one of the jurors could neither read nor write-he was immediately accepted by Darrow. The incident involving Drummond's suspenders also occurred at Dayton. The reference by Brady to the obscenity controversy in the Endicott case, though, has no historical relationship to Clarence Darrow. The objection to the "Read Your Bible" sign, however, was made by Darrow and, unlike the sign in the play it was removed. In none of these instances, though, did Lawrence and Lee borrow any phrases from the trial transcripts; in each case the dialogue is their own.

Act Two, Scene One. Brady's statement to the reporters that Drummond supported him in his 1908 campaign for the presidency bears a distinct relationship to the fact that in 1896 Clarence Darrow, as a Democratic candidate for the Illinois legislature, did support, though not actively, William Jennings Bryan in his campaign. (Both were defeated.) The prayer meeting scene and the incident between the fictitious Reverend Brown and Brady is a total creation of the playwrights' imaginations.

Act Two Scene Two. The playwrights return to the trial for the testimony of Howard Blair, who, as did Howard Morgan, explained to the court what Cates (Scopes) had taught him concerning the theory of evolution. Brady's remark about being descended "from good American monkeys" occurred in a similar form in the Scopes trial. Drummond's remarks to Howard about his baseball game were not a part of the original trial, but reflect Lawrence and Lee's diligent research, for Clarence Darrow had once been an avid baseball fan and player.

While Rachel's testimony and breakdown are wholly fictitious, Lawrence and Lee follow the pattern of the most dramatic incident of the trial - the questioning of Bryan by Clarence Darrow. The fact that Darrow had brought to Dayton fifteen noted scientists to testify in behalf of his client and the theory of evolution, only to have the prosecution objections sustained by the judge, is preserved in *Inherit the Wind*. As in the play, the defense, in a surprising move, then called William Jennings Bryan to the stand.

As in the play, Bryan's fellow prosecutor Tom Stewart objected, but Bryan, like Brady, chose to testify. Darrow opened by attempting to establish Bryan as an expert on the Bible, questioned him on the story of Jonah, Joshua and the sun, the Bible's dating of the creation and the flood, Cain and his wife, and the length of the first three "days" of creation. Lawrence and Lee, however, restrain themselves from using more than a few phrases from the actual transcripts; major speeches, such as Drummond's Truth versus Right speech, are entirely their creation.

Act Three, Scene One. Lawrence and Lee inject into the third and final act of their play the presence of the radio man, who is part of the first remote broadcast of a trial. Historically, the radio broadcast, which did establish a radio "first," had begun on the opening day of the trial, but the playwrights save it until the third act to heighten the interest in the verdict and sentencing.

The guilty verdict reflects the actual outcome of the original trial, as does the judge's error in forgetting to allow Cates to make a statement prior to his sentencing. Just as Darrow did at Dayton, Drummond corrects the judge in the play, and Cates begins his pledge to continue to fight the anti-evolution law. Portions of his speech, but not the interruption by Mrs. Krebbs, are accurate recreations of Scopes' actual statement. In both instances the fine was one hundred dollars, but, unlike that in the play, the actual punishment was limited to a maximum of five hundred dollars and no jail sentence. Lawrence and Lee, though, imply that Cates could possibly be sent to prison in order to create and maintain suspense, and to contrast the judge's fine with Brady's expectations. Historically, the jury, not the mayor, indicated that John T. Scopes should be fined the minimum amount - one hundred dollars.

In Dayton, Bryan was prevented from making a final address to the jury by Darrow, who waived the defense's right (and thus the prosecution's) to a closing summation in order to keep Bryan from delivering his carefully prepared speech. Brady's collapse in court, however, was initiated by the playwrights to condense the action and symbolize his defeat and that of Fundamentalism. William Jennings Bryan actually died quite unexpectedly five days later while still in Dayton. Hornbeck's line -"[he] died of a busted belly" - was actually Clarence Darrow's, but the playwrights changed the source to remain consistent to the character of Henry Drummond. Finally, two other factual items from the trial appear in the play, both involving money. First, Mencken's newspaper did post bond for John T. Scopes as is indicated in the play, and, second, Clarence Darrow did defend Scopes without accepting any payment for his services.

The Scopes Monkey Trial of July, 1925, did indeed provide playwrights Jerome Lawrence and Robert E. Lee with a general structure and story line on which they based *Inherit the Wind*, but they created new characters and dialogue, and arranged the action to give the play dramatic intensity - something the trial did not always have. Consequently, *Inherit the Wind* does not depend upon the Scopes Trial, but grows from it and flourishes as a unique and valuable work in its own right.

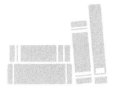

INHERIT THE WIND

....

HOWARD BLAIR

The thirteen-year-old student of Bert Cates exemplifies all of the characteristics of a young boy growing up in a small country town, who is suddenly caught up in the furor over teaching the theory of evolution in the public schools. As the opening scene reveals, Howard has not understood all that Cates has taught him, but he is called to testify at the trial. Unlike many of the adults in Hillsboro, Howard reveals on the stand his honesty and openness, and is unafraid to admit that he does not understand all that Drummond and Brady have said. On three occasions in the play it is young Howard Blair who, in his open and almost naive manner, sees things as they truly are: first, it is Howard who realizes that the preparations for Brady and the trial appear more like the preparations for the "county fair"; second, it is Howard who first comes to believe in Henry Drummond; third, it is Howard who admits after the trial is concluded that he does not know who won. The total effect of the trial, and, more specifically, Drummond's lessons on evolution, education, the Bible, and freedom of speech, will not be reflected in the adults of Hillsboro as they will in the children like Howard Blair who are willing to listen to both sides before making up their minds, and who, thus, are the hope for the future.

RACHEL BROWN

Although each of the major characters in the play must struggle with some form of conflict, Rachel Brown, the daughter of a Fundamentalist minister and girlfriend of the community evolutionist, suffers the most difficult conflict and, consequently, undergoes the greatest change. In the course of the action Rachel develops from a naive, conforming country girl into an independent, assertive young woman.

Sources of Rachel's conflicts are her father and the Hillsboro environment in which she has been raised. Trained to respect and fear him, she is ever-conscious of the impression she makes on her father's parishioners. It is not until she betrays Bert, and yet is singled out and rejected by her father, that she begins to realize how little control she has over either her mind or her life. Henry Drummond and Bert Cates, both through word and example, inspire Rachel to rebel against the mold her father and the townspeople have been forcing her into. Her reading of *Origin of Species* (though, as she admits, she did not understand much of it) symbolizes her new self-awareness and independence, as does her decision to leave Hillsboro and her father. As if to emphasize her independence, Lawrence and Lee are careful not to give any indication that Rachel is now dependent on Bert for her survival. Her decision to leave has been made without him and it is only on her way to the train station that she stops to apologize to him. His decision to set out with her leaves no doubt in the mind of the audience of the value the trial has had for both of them

BERT CATES

Although a central figure in the evolution controversy, Bert Cates emerges as a minor figure in the battle between Drummond and Brady. Throughout the play he remains consistent: shy, kind, considerate of others, yet a man of principle, who, though he has inadvertently stirred up a great deal of commotion that awes him, never seriously considers, even under extreme pressure, abandoning the fight for freedom of speech both in and out of the classroom.

Cates loses control of his temper only once during the trial, that being during the testimony of Rachel's describing her father's handling of the Stebbins boy's funeral. Not unlike the tone of the attack he made on Cates and Rachel during the prayer meeting, the Reverend Brown's funeral oration resulted in Cates' departure from the church.

But even after all that Matthew Harrison Brady has said about him in public and tried to do to him, Bert Cates does not rejoice in his death. He holds, from the opening scene to his final exit, the respect of all who sit in the audience and watch him

REVEREND JEREMIAH BROWN

Jerome Lawrence and Robert E. Lee have the unusual ability to make even their unpopular and villainous characters human and, thus, sympathetic. Even Reverend Brown, who relies on power and fear to control the townspeople of Hillsboro, gains a degree of pity when in his fanatic passion to destroy all defenders of the theory of evolution, he destroys his following and the remains of his family. Highly emotional and never happy, Brown is quick to anger - and quick to convince the townspeople that Henry Drummond is an agent of the devil. Lawrence and Lee's skilled craftsmanship is evidenced in their careful construction of his character. Remarks such as "We won't let him [Drummond] in the town" and "I always like to begin my meetings at the time announced" reveal his lack of reason and his tendency towards inflexibility, both of which later combine at the prayer meeting to destroy his effectiveness. Although the focus of attention is on his daughter, perhaps Brown's final action in the play - removing Rachel from the witness stand after her testimony - is the most sympathetic, for he reflects no change in his character; he shows no evidence of any acknowledgment of his error in judgment at the prayer meeting; and he gives no indication of changing to meet the new needs of the townspeople or of his daughter.

E. K. HORNBECK

Although he is on assignment from the Baltimore Herald, E. K. Hornbeck claims to be not a reporter but a critic. Nor does he pretend to be unbiased, for he is a devoted cynic who is openly contemptuous of the people of Hillsboro and their exalted leader, Matthew Harrison Brady. He uses as his main weapon barbed sarcasm, with which he prods the townspeople and Brady whenever he is given the opportunity. It is not enough, though, for him to be a critic, for he also plays the role of philosopher, prophet, and poet. He is a good newspaperman in that he is an observer of people, is perceptive and blunt, and has an eye for the unusual, as evidenced by his final story on the trial. Yet he speaks like a poet and enjoys quoting from Shakespeare, Tennyson, and Sandburg. He admires his own writing, but, in spite of this, does not hold himself aloof from his own cynicism. But Hornbeck is not too harsh on himself, and one of the reasons he so dislikes Matthew Harrison Brady may be perhaps that he sees in the Great Commoner something that he detests, even in himself - vanity.

The one person in Hillsboro with whom Hornbeck can feel a degree of affinity is Henry Drummond, but he mistakenly believes that the way to gain the praise, respect, and friendship of Drummond is to make Hillsboro and Brady the butt of his jokes. Drummond is unimpressed, however, and ignores him until Hornbeck attacks the deceased Brady. Hornbeck is stunned when Drummond turns on him, and the critic from Baltimore defends himself with snarling sarcasm. Although he comes the closest of all the people in Hillsboro to truly understanding Henry Drummond and perceiving the real reason for Brady's presence, there is a distinct difference between Hornbeck and Drummond that becomes surprisingly clear near the close of the play. Unlike Drummond, Hornberck cannot separate the sin from the sinner, and since he hates the ideas that Brady supports, he in turn hates Brady. He cannot understand how Drummond, after Brady's scathing attacks on him, can defend and praise the man. Rather than understand it, Hornbeck labels Drummond a hypocrite and it becomes evident that E.K. Hornbeck has become so involved with being a cynic that he ceases to be a human being.

MATTHEW HARRISON BRADY

In order to prepare the audience for his entrance and to indicate his importance in the play, playwrights Lawrence and Lee use the townspeople to begin Brady's characterization. Before he arrives, the audience knows that he has an indomitable spirit, a loud voice, and a reputation as defender of the faith and the common man. His appearance (balding, paunchy, sixty-five years old), his reference to the heat, and his limitless appetite foreshadow his eventual death, but are overshadowed at first by his smooth, persuasive style of speaking. His conversations with the local officials reflect the ease with which he adapts to the new situation and the familiarity he feels amongst the townspeople of Hillsboro. Sensing the opportunity Rachel's naivete presents, he wisely slips away with her to garner information for his case by convincing her that he is her friend. Even the discovery of the forthcoming arrival of the famous Henry Drummond cannot dampen his enthusiasm; unlike the others, he welcomes the opportunity to battle the opposition's best lawyer and reflects the confidence he always adheres to in himself.

The jury selection scene offers the audience further insight into Brady's character. The famous orator expects the "show" to be his, but his mind is not as agile as his opponent's, and he finds himself being laughed at occasionally. His two greatest concerns are that the members of the jury chosen to sit in judgment of Bert Cates conform to society's standards, and that Drummond not be allowed to confuse them - as he has done other juries.

The prayer meeting scene reveals Brady at his best - charming, personable, sincere, and rational. Brown's extreme emotionalism stirs Brady not to join in the condemnation of the two young people, but to ask the townspeople to forgive them and Brown. Gently, yet firmly, he takes control of the crowd, but cannot sway Drummond, who accuses him of living in the past.

Brady's carefully constructed prosecution and his objection to Drummond's scientific witnesses secure a guilty verdict for Bert Cates, but his vanity and overconfidence cause him to lose the battle with Henry Drummond. Spurred onto the stand by his greed for additional glory, Brady resembles a lumbering bear, who battles with sheer power and force, beset by Drummond the fox who continually circles him, nipping away at his exposed flanks, enraging, confusing, and gradually destroying him in the process. From the gallant warrior he is reduced to a sobbing, broken old man, for under the scalpel-like questioning of Henry Drummond his bombast and rhetoric fall aside, laying bare his lack of intelligence and reason.

Yet as he did at the picnic, Brady quickly recovers, though in a more subdued manner, the following day. His frustration at the sentence, the townspeople, and himself - complicated by his sensitivity to the heat and his addiction to food - climaxes in his collapse and ensuing death. Much like the Reverend Brown's, Brady's intentions were noble, but misdirected and outdated. He neglects to realize that his beliefs and his dwindling number of followers were rapidly becoming a part of the stagnant past. Not unlike the towering dinosaur who once roamed and ruled the land, Brady fails to adapt to the changing environment and thus is destroyed by it.

TOM DAVENPORT

The young circuit district attorney finds himself in the uncomfortable and unfortunate situation of always standing in the shadow of Matthew Harrison Brady. Technically, the position of head of the state's prosecution was his, and it should have followed that the fame contingent with the trial would have been his as well, but Brady's entrance transfixes him into a resigned and submissive subordinate. Nevertheless, Davenport is sharp, quick, and perceptive; he senses before Brady the trap Henry Drummond has baited, but cannot interpose upon his superior to prevent him from taking the stand. His worst fears are quickly realized, and the young district attorney must sit helplessly by as their victory in court is marred by his fellow lawyer.

SARAH BRADY

The most devoted disciple of Matthew Harrison Brady, orator, politician, and lawyer, is without a doubt his wife Sarah. Her whole life revolves around that of her husband and, with little or no regard for her own well-being, she constantly strives to protect him from his most dangerous enemy - himself. The perfect politician's mate - well-dressed, devoted, and unassuming - she fights to stay out of the limelight and headlines. When photographers converge upon them, she would slip a few feet away; yet never did she venture so far as to not be able to correct a pose that might cast a poor reflection on her husband. She alone knew how fragile this giant of a man was; although Brady ignored it, she did not. During their stay in Hillsboro she chides him for eating too much, ignoring his doctor's orders, and becoming overheated; he affectionately calls her "Mother" to show his appreciation for her concern. But her advice goes unheeded, and, in the end, Sarah Brady finds herself a widow.

THE JUDGE

A principal figure in the trial but a minor character in the play, the judge reveals himself to be little more than one of the townspeople with a robe on. Whenever he becomes confused by the furor of the two vocal lawyers, he looks to Brady for guidance; yet, ironically, he allows Brady to place himself at Drummond's mercy when he could - and should - have prevented Drummond from straying so far from the actual question at hand.

THE TOWNSPEOPLE

Naive, honest, simple, the Hillsboro residents strongly endorse Brady and Fundamentalism as the play opens. Foremost in their minds, though, is not justice, but financial reward for themselves as a result of the trial. Their admiration for Brady reaches heroic proportions - especially after they reject the Reverend Brown for attacking Bert Cates and his daughter at the prayer meeting. The meeting reflects their attitude toward religion: they stand obediently before their leader, imitate his actions, and give predetermined responses. They are not devoid of the ability to think for themselves, though, as evidenced by their refusal to support Brown at the close of the meeting.

The trial is effectively used by Drummond to educate the people of Hillsboro, and as it progresses the change in the attitude of the spectators can be traced. The number of "Amens" diminishes as the applause for Drummond increases. Although they never fully desert their materialistic desires, by the close of the trial they have lost their faith in Brady as well as in the Reverend Brown, and have begun, for the first time, to think about religion and evolution.

The people of Hillsboro are similar to many persons in many small towns. Generally, they are not highly educated, conform to society's standards, and tend to be close-minded; yet they excel in kindness, sincerity, honesty, and can think and act independently. They can give and take their attention and support at will, depending, at times, upon the oratorical powers of the speaker before them.

HENRY DRUMMOND

The agnostic, unorthodox lawyer from Chicago emerges as the play's most individualistic character. Sharp-witted, cunning courtroom tactician, quick-thinking, Drummond appears sincere, open, honest, and friendly. Unlike the townspeople, he cannot be influenced by money, and he is a man of high principles. Although he does not endorse organized religion, he knows the Bible well. Language is his tool, and unlike Brady and Hornbeck who also employ it, Drummond can adjust it to the situation and audience he faces. Drummond's knowledge of people enables him to stand back and view the proceedings at Hillsboro with an objective eye, and he is able to sense the long-range damage that could be done to enlightenment and progress if Brady and the Fundamentalists were allowed to affect the education of America's youth. Drummond directs his life in the search for Truth, and, consequently, oftentimes disregards society's label of Right. As an individual, a nonconformist, he normally stands alone in his fight to preserve such rights as the freedom of speech and the right, as he says, "to be wrong."

INHERIT THE WIND

. . . .

HISTORY OF INHERIT THE WIND

When Jerome Lawrence and Robert E. Lee first began collaborating in 1942, both were deeply involved in radio: Lee as a director for the radio advertising firm of Young and Rubicam, and Lawrence as a writer with CBS. One of their first discussions centered on the evolution trial at Dayton, but the war and their work with the Armed Forces Radio Service prevented them from writing *Inherit the Wind.* After the war, as the team of Lawrence and Lee continued to write for radio and began work on their first musical, *Look, Ma, I'm Dancin',* their plans for a play revolving around the Scopes Trial were set aside, but not forgotten. The actions of Senator Joseph McCarthy early in 1950, however, suddenly provided Lawrence and Lee with the needed impetus for the creation of *Inherit the Wind.*

McCarthyism. On February 9, 1950, in a speech delivered in Wheeling, West Virginia, a first-year Republican senator from Wisconsin, Joseph R. McCarthy, announced that he had in his possession the names of fifty-seven "card-carrying Communists" working in the State Department.

McCarthy's accusations fanned the flames of postwar fear and suspicion in the United States into a roaring blaze. The Cold War struggle between the Communist and Western nations after World War II and the growing mistrust in the Truman administration had made the American people fearful of Communist infiltration and the possible overthrow of democracy. Joseph McCarthy rose to charge the Truman and the former Roosevelt administrations with "treason" and demanded that the Democratic administration currently in office be purged of all Communist sympathizers.

A Senate investigation into McCarthy's original charges revealed that the Senator had no proof to back his accusations, yet with the support of a growing number of conservatives, McCarthy kept his Communist "witch-hunt" alive. After reelection in 1952, McCarthy became chairman of the powerful Permanent Subcommittee on Investigation - a post which accorded him the power to investigate anyone whom he suspected of being a Communist, subversive, or threat to the American government.

Although Eisenhower had begrudgingly supported McCarthy in his successful bid for reelection, the new President found his own administration under investigation by the Senator's committee. McCarthy accused Eisenhower, along with Roosevelt and Truman, of being a traitor to his country, and labeled Secretary of state Dean Acheson and other prominent public officials as "un-American." Those who dared criticize or oppose the McCarthy investigations often found their own backgrounds and associations being scrutinized. McCarthy's supporters, often backed by wealthy rightwingers, ruined the careers of thousands of liberals and reformers in government, education, and entertainment. College professors, writers, broadcasters, actors, television, film, and radio personalities lost their jobs and had their reputations destroyed by "guilt by association" or mere suspicion.

From April 22 to June 17, 1954, the McCarthy hearings were broadcast over national television, and millions of people began to realize that McCarthy's malicious methods of investigation were not justified by conclusive results. His baseless charges and investigative procedures caused his colleagues to level charges against him; on December 2, 1954, by a vote of 67 to 22, the Senate voted to censure Senator Joseph R. McCarthy.

The central question that arose from the McCarthy investigation was whether or not Communists, or any American citizen who happens to be a critic of the democratic form of government, could claim the right to freedom of speech as guaranteed in the United States Constitution. McCarthy did not believe that they could, nor did thousands of people who supported him and his cause. As a result, although McCarthyism did increase security precautions within the government and threatened actual subversives, it also marred America's reputation as a "free" country, damaged the lives of innocent people, lowered the morale and efficiency of the State Department, and created an atmosphere of fear and suspicion throughout the country.

DRAMATIC STRUCTURE AND TECHNIQUE

Setting, Time, And Cast Of Characters. Before the curtain rises on the first scene, the playwright has at his disposal three opportunities to prepare the audience or reader for the action they are about to witness. The setting of the action can convey more than simply the geographical location of the play: in the case of *Inherit the Wind* the playwrights are purposely evasive in confining the action to one particular place. The stage direction, "a small town," prevents the viewer from associating the action of the play with one geographical region, just as the time "summer

- not too long ago," circumvents any attempt to tie the action to one particular time period. Subsequently, the playwrights are able to indicate to their audience before the play begins that they are not attempting to document one particular incident which took place at one particular time in history. Instead, the play assumes a relevance to almost any geographical location at almost any time - including today or tomorrow. (Students may be familiar with Shirley Jackson's implementation of neutral setting in her short story "The Lottery" and its relationship to the **theme** of that particular work.)

Yet the playwrights' directions for the setting of the play do more than prevent the viewer from associating the action with any particular town or area. Even the deceptively simple direction "a small town" carries with it certain inherent values: the type of people associated with a small town, their occupations, mode of life, religious beliefs, degree of education, and social behavior. All of these within even the most simple stage direction, and each has a valuable relationship to the effectiveness of the play.

The astute viewer, whether he be a member of an audience or a student in a class, can take advantage of the playwright's cast of characters. A quick scan of the cast of *Inherit the Wind* reveals an abundance of rather common names - highly appropriate for the members of a small, country community. A few names stand out - the Reverend Jeremiah Brown, E.K. Hornbeck (the only character who uses his initials in place of his first name), and Matthew Harrison Brady (the only character whose middle name is spelled out); the presence of a judge, jurors, reporters, hawkers (including a hotdog man and a hurdy-gurdy grinder), and spectators add yet another dimension to the viewers' expectations before the rise of the curtain.

ACT ONE

Unlike the novelist or biographer, the playwright works under strict time limitations. For that reason he must take advantage of every line and action from the opening curtain to the final drop. In addition, he knows that every night his play must entertain hundreds of persons who come to the theatre with little or nothing in common. Many, if not most, he can assume, will know little more than the title of his work and perhaps the basic plot line. The playwright, then, must quickly accomplish a variety of tasks in order to catch the attention of his audience, introduce them to his characters and the situation surrounding them, and carry the audience and his characters forward into the action.

By the close of the first act, the playwright must have set the tone of the action on the stage and created an atmosphere for his audience. They must sense whether the play is a tragedy, a comedy, a melodrama, a problem play, etc., in order that they may adjust their expectations and reactions accordingly. In addition, the playwright must inform his viewers of that which has taken place prior to the opening curtain and prepare them for that which is about to take place. This **exposition**, as it is called, is made necessary by the belief, first expressed by Aristotle, that a good play begins "in the middle of things," and is judged "well constructed" when it not only informs the audience of past events and information, but moves the action of the play forward as well. Also in the first act the playwright must either introduce the characters or prepare the audience for their entrances. Simultaneously, he will begin the rising action and build suspense, usually through emerging conflicts and subsequent complications to these conflicts.

Scene One

Howard and Melinda. Since they are working under rather rigid time restrictions, playwrights are limited to the number of characters whom they can adequately create, explore, and motivate in the course of their play. For that reason they sometimes employ stock or stereotype characters for a variety of purposes. Lawrence and Lee open *Inherit the Wind* with two such characters, Howard and Melinda, in order that they might help set the tone and create an atmosphere for the forthcoming action. The stage directions describe them as all-American children with pigtails, fishing pole, and worms. Recognizing them as such, the audience completes their characterization, thus relieving the playwrights of the time-consuming responsibility of creating and motivating entirely unique characters.

Howard's misinterpretation of Darwin's theory of evolution and Melinda's reaction to it as "sinful" reflect the extent to which the controversy over evolution has infiltrated the lives of the people of Hillsboro. Although neither completely understands why, Howard and Melinda find themselves in conflict, and the viewer prepares himself to watch how the conflict between the forces of evolution and those of religion affect the people of Hillsboro. The language with which the playwrights supply Howard and Melinda reflects their small country-town environment and is highly appropriate to them. The **irony** of the situation becomes painfully clear when the viewer realizes that one of the major concerns in the play is the teaching of evolution to schoolchildren, yet the audience notices before the townspeople that Howard has actually understood little of what he was taught.

Although their time on stage is brief, Howard and Melinda serve as comic figures in order to establish a light and humorous tone, and, at the same time, foreshadow the approach of a highly serious problem.

Rachel's Visit to the Jail. Although the brief interchange between Howard and Melinda helped establish the play's central conflict while entertaining and relaxing the audience, it did not (nor was it intended to) supply any of the needed **exposition**. Rachel's conversations with Mr. Meeker, the bailiff, and Bert Cates at the courthouse jail, though, provide the audience with background information and introduce conflicts, complications, and suspense.

The stage directions prior to Rachel's first lines interject the play's first elements of suspense, which continue to build as the action of the play moves forward. Her nervousness and distress, combined with the possibility that she has been crying and her concern that she not be seen approaching the jail, fuse to instill in the minds of the audience members a degree of inquisitiveness. Her first concern - that her father not be told that she had come to the jail - heightens the tension and discloses a clue to her relationship with him. Mr. Meeker's response also provides a reflection upon the Reverend Brown's character and prepares the audience for his eventual entrance. Meeker, who represents the Hillsboro people, also provides the audience with information vital to their understanding of the play; he divulges that Bert Cates, a local school-teacher, is locked up in the town jail and, although he does not reveal why, he supplies the audience with comic relief as he recollects memories of past prisoners. Like young Howard Blair, his language reflects his environment - his dropping of the subject in his sentences, his slurring of words and the ending of -ing, and his general economy of words. Inherent in Mr. Meeker is the quality of trust; just as Rachel is assured that he will not reveal her whereabouts to her father, he is able to trust her and Cates alone outside the jail.

Rachel's conversation with Bert Cates serves two major purposes: first, it is the play's major piece of **exposition**, and, second, it provides the inciting force of the play's action. Within a few lines the audience can sense the close relationship Rachel and Bert have, and discover precisely why he is in jail, who is coming to prosecute him, how the townspeople feel about what he has done, and even exactly what he taught his students about the theory of evolution. Lawrence and Lee skillfully weave this vital information into their characters' conversations while in all but one case continuously moving the action forward. The only instance of strained **exposition** occurs when Bert explains the details of his evolution lesson to Rachel, who, as a teacher and close friend, would undoubtedly already be familiar with them. The miniature lesson on Darwin's theory, though, was designed by Lawrence and Lee not for Rachel, but for their audience, whom they could not safely presume correctly understood the theory of evolution and whom they could not leave with Howard's explanation. Yet it must also be pointed out that Lawrence and Lee use this particular piece of dialogue to introduce one of the play's central ideas - that the theory of evolution and the Biblical account of creation are not necessarily irreconcilable.

Technically, the inciting force that inspired Bert Cates to challenge the law banning the theory of evolution from the classroom occurred before the play opened, but Rachel, with her plea for him to admit his guilt and avoid the controversy, indirectly compels him to reaffirm his commitment to fight what he considers an unjust law. Her plea, combined with her obvious sensitivity to the opinions of the other townspeople and the fact that she is the local minister's daughter, adds complications to the conflicts they both already face. At this point in the play the audience can begin to understand the dilemma that Rachel, as the local minister's daughter and girlfriend of the evolutionist schoolteacher, is forced to struggle with. The fact that the audience witnesses her attempt to convince Bert - but not her father - to change his views indicates either that she cannot easily approach her father, or that she already knows that he will not change.

Meeker's return and his subsequent dialogue with Cates serve as the preparatory transition from the jail scene to the arrival of Matthew Harrison Brady. His glowing description of the power and ability of the man who is coming to prosecute Bert Cates darkens the defendant's hopes - especially when it becomes apparent that he does not know who is coming to defend him. In his preoccupation with Brady's arrival, Meeker fails to remember or realize that Cates would not share his enthusiasm over Brady. For Meeker at least, Matthew Harrison Brady's visit to Hillsboro seems to be far more important than the reason for his journey - Bert Cates' trial.

Brady's Arrival. After Meeker's preliminary preparation for the entrance of Matthew Harrison Brady onto the stage, playwrights Lawrence and Lee build interest and suspense through the dialogue and actions of the people of Hillsboro. Mrs. Krebbs and Mr. Goodfellow (appropriate names) emphasize the ever-present heat and, more importantly, the fundamental religious beliefs of the townspeople. Mrs. Krebbs especially symbolizes their beliefs with her inability to preface the word "Lord" with anything but the adjective "Good." Previous remarks by Rachel, Meeker, and Cates anticipated the entrance of the Reverend Jeremiah Brown, whose manner immediately explains why Rachel fears him. It is evident that Brown is in control of the townspeople as they prepare for Brady's arrival, and his overconcern heightens interest and emphasizes the importance of the great orator's visit to them. Lawrence and Lee, though, cleverly employ Brown as a vehicle of dramatic **irony**, for when he implores the townspeople to show Brady "what kind of community this is" he does not realize that his words carry a double meaning for the viewers. In addition to preparing the audience for Brady's entrance, the townspeople unwittingly reveal an insight into their character and motivation - the desire for money. Cates, the trial, and the theory of evolution are never mentioned; crowds, business, and money occupy their minds. As Howard indicates, the town has been transformed into a setting for a county fair rather than a trial: lemonade, fans, and Bibles go on sale in the rush to take advantage of the attention brought to bear on Hillsboro by the trial and the arrival of Matthew Harrison Brady.

After effectively establishing the basic character of the people of Hillsboro, Lawrence and Lee provide the audience with a foil and contrast to them through the unheralded entrance of a reporter from Baltimore - E.K. Hornbeck. The cynical reporter's rapier-like wit pares away at the thinly disguised materialism and backwoods ishness that pervade the rather simple and naive townspeople and permits the audience to sit in judgment on them. Simultaneously, the playwrights reveal Hornbeck's character through his language; his blunt criticism of the townspeople and of their hero Matthew Harrison Brady, his lack of concern for the opinions others hold of him, and his love for words, as evidenced by his use of puns (monkey and "monkeyshines") and **alliteration** ("the buckle on the Bible Belt,") combine to establish the cynical critic's character. His brief soliloquy, as the townspeople flock to the train station singing "Marching to Zion," presents the audience with yet another and contrasting opinion of Matthew Harrison Brady, for Hornbeck lacks the fervent hero-worship of the people of Hillsboro. Sarcastically, Hornbeck addresses his description - which also heightens audience anticipation to actually see Brady - to the hurdy-gurdy monkey, the unfortunate symbol of evolution to those seeking a simplistic interpretation. His brief conversation with Goodfellow emphasizes what has already been made clear: the people of Hillsboro are more interested in business than in the principles at stake in the trial.

The timing of Hornbeck's entrance was carefully planned to follow and contrast the paramount view held by Meeker, Bollinger, and the other townspeople of Matthew Harrison Brady, and to immediately precede Brady's first appearance on stage. Consequently, the playwrights, by presenting their audience with conflicting descriptions of the great orator, coerce them into focusing their attention on him in order to decide which, if either, is closer to his true character.

Brady's arrival is preceded by the townspeople singing "Gimme That Old Time Religion" - highly appropriate for his entry - and it is interesting to note the contrast in the language between the townspeople and Brady. Outside of the Reverend Brown (whose language reflects his education), their diction and **syntax** represent that of the roughshod - neither illiterate nor intellectually astute - while Brady speaks with the smoothness of an experienced and educated orator. Even in his first few lines, the playwrights begin unobtrusively to foreshadow his eventual death with his discomfort under the glaring sun and his infatuation with food (the latter of which also supplies the play with some of its best humor). Brady, the experienced politician, is at ease amongst those who worship him and is wise enough to overlook their awkward attempts to welcome him to their community. The sincere but humorous efforts on the part of the mayor to formally greet and introduce him produce, as did Meeker earlier, comic relief for the audience which is intent on assessing Brady's character. Just as the townspeople have multiple interests in the trial and its effect on their town, Brady reveals that he, too, has more in mind than the prosecution of Bert Cates. The attention he (and Mrs. Brady) bring to bear on the photographer in the midst of the mayor's speech and his reference to the "big cities in the North" reflect his desire to gain attention and notoriety from the trial.

The major complication to Bert Cates' conflict with the law emerges when Brady inquires as to his character and Rachel instinctively comes to his defense. Her naivete blindly leads her to confide in Brady, yet Lawrence and Lee withhold from the audience the actual context of their conversation in order to heighten interest and build suspense. Simultaneously, Hornbeck's entrance moves the action of the play forward and complicates Brady's prosecution efforts with the announcement of the defense lawyer - "the most agile legal mind in the world today - Henry Drummond." As they did with Brown and Brady, Lawrence and Lee present the audience with contradictory opinions of Drummond prior to his entrance. The resulting paradox creates the desired effect - interest and suspense surrounds the anticipated entrance of the lawyer from Chicago. Mrs. Brady especially serves as a litmus to Drummond's reputation, and the Reverend Brown's devil **imagery** effectively establishes a foreboding tone. Brady's reaction to the announcement increases interest in Drummond and reinforces the complication the lawyer's participation in the trial will add to Brady's attempts to prosecute Cates. But Brady's discovery is marked by seemingly unconquerable optimism and confidence as he recognizes the additional attention that will be heaped upon him as he defeats Bert Cates, the theory of evolution, and Henry Drummond. Finally, Brady foreshadows Drummond's trial tactics of placing the law on trial in place of the defendant, and reminds the audience of his new and important witness, Rachel Brown.

Lawrence and Lee close this tense, highly emotional scene with Mrs. Brady's insistence that her husband take a nap and with yet another comical reference to his boundless appetite - both of which foreshadow future trouble for him. The townspeople leave with him just as they had met him, singing "Gimme That Old Time Religion."

Rachel and Hornbeck. The conversation between Rachel and Hornbeck in the courtroom outside the jail emphasizes the conflict raging within her and increases audience interest in that which she confided to Brady. It also, through **diction** and **syntax**, reveals more of the character of Hornbeck. Yet more importantly, it exposes much of the philosophy that Rachel and most of the townspeople of Hillsboro hold fast to, especially concerning teachers, evolution, and the Bible, and it presents an open and uncomplimentary view of Brady and his motivation for coming to Hillsboro. The audience is faced with two attitudes toward Brady: blind devotion to the defender of the faith and the protector of the common man, and cynical skepticism towards a loud relic of the past.

Drummond's Entrance. One of the most dramatically effective moments of the play is marked by the entrance of Henry Drummond. The Playwrights prepared the audience for his arrival with descriptions laced with devil analogies from Reverend Brown, horror from Mrs. Brady, and comparisons from Brady matching Drummond with Goliath and the dragon slain by St. George. The red sunset, huge, slouching shadow, and screams from Melinda reinforce the devil **imagery** associated earlier with Drummond, heighten emotional suspense, and draw the conflict into symbolic focus: Brady, the gallant defender of the faith, versus Drummond, the agnostic agent of darkness.

Scene Two

Jury Selection. As the action of the play switches to the actual trial a few days later, the stage directions of the second scene emphasize two things: the heat, which has partly accounted for the moving of the court to the courthouse lawn, and the fact that the townspeople are also on trial in the play. After the rather serious tone in the latter half of the first scene, the jury selection scene offers the play's greatest number of humorous lines and situations. Lawrence and Lee, though, do more than entertain their audience; they give them their first close look at Henry Drummond, the agnostic lawyer from Chicago. In contrast to the devil **imagery** associated with him in the previous scene, Drummond appears as friendly and easygoing as a small-town shopkeeper; his language is unlike that of Brady or someone associated with a city like Chicago. Instead, Henry Drummond speaks the language of the people of Hillsboro. The conflict between the two great lawyers quickly emerges and grows as they trade quips concerning Drummond's suspenders, an objection to Brady's title, and a key issue in the trial - legislative control of public-school teachers. As a prelude to the coming battle, the first skirmish between the two "colonels" results in simultaneous outbursts from both sides of the aisle.

The playwrights make a subtle transition from the action in the court to the forthcoming prayer meeting by having the judge announce it at the close of the jury selection. Drummond's objection to the announcement and to the "Read Your Bible" sign incites the judge and, by the time that court has adjourned for the day, Drummond has inflamed the prosecution and the townspeople as well - all of which was designed by the playwrights to increase suspense and interest, and to heighten the conflict between the unorthodox Henry Drummond and almost everyone in the court.

An interesting contrast between the styles of the two lawyers is made more evident by their respective use of language. Brady's **diction** and **syntax** - "Unless the state of mind of the members of the jury conforms to the laws and patterns of society..." - clearly reflect his training in law, politics, and public speaking, but also isolate him from the townspeople of Hillsboro. On the other hand, Drummond, a skillful courtroom tactician and student of human psychology, attempts to bridge the gulf of ideas that separates him from the townspeople by speaking their style of language - "Tell me, Mr. Sillers...did you ever happen to bump into a fella named Charles Darwin?" The results are not immediate, however, and the townspeople still strongly support Brady and the prosecution after the final juror is selected.

Rachel, Cates, and Drummond. Although the shouting has died down, the conflicts within the play have not, and Lawrence and Lee deftly focus the attention of the audience back to the almost forgotten defendant, Bert Cates. Once again, the audience watches as Cates wrestles with his dilemma; Rachel implores him to admit his guilt, yet as a man of principle he does not want to submit to the pressure of the townspeople to conform. Complications quickly add to his problem: Rachel is concerned about how the townspeople feel about him, but is more concerned with the knowledge that Brady will call her to the stand. Although he has already reaffirmed his decision to continue with the trial against almost insurmountable odds, Cates panics at the thought of Rachel testifying to some of the things he had said to her in private. His reaction confirms what Lawrence and Lee have led the audience to suspect: Rachel's testimony will destroy what little chance he had to gain an acquittal. Thus Lawrence and Lee make the transition to the next trial scene, yet they are careful not to reveal to the audience at this point exactly what Rachel will be called upon to say.

Cates' exit with Meeker leads into Drummond's discovery of Rachel's relationship to the Reverend Brown and the emergence of the play's primary subplot: Rachel's relationship with her father and the effect which it has on her. His character has, by the close of this act, been established by his actions, his words, and by what others have said about him, and Rachel's confession to Drummond after Bert's departure heightens the conflict within the subplot and draws attention to her struggle to gain identity and independence.

ACT TWO

After setting the tone, introducing the characters, establishing the **exposition**, and revealing the major conflicts and complications in the first act, the playwrights turn their attention in the second act to the rising action and additional complications. In addition, the turning point of the action may occur, as well as the most exciting point in the play, the climax.

Scene One

Prayer Meeting. Playwrights Lawrence and Lee began the transition from the trial proceedings to the prayer meeting with the judge's announcement in the final scene of the first act and with Rachel's narrative description of the Reverend Brown. As in each of the previous two scenes, they open the action with the townspeople, thus never allowing the audience to forget that they, too, are on trial. The dialogue between Sillers and Dunlap concerning the "Read Your Bible" sign indicates that after the jury selection the townspeople are still clearly behind Brady, and Henry Drummond still retains his label as the Devil.

The brief press conference between Brady and the reporters serves as a reminder to the theatre audience of the importance of the trial and of the attention being focused upon it, even by the London papers. The playwrights also reveal more of the character of Matthew Harrison Brady, the politician. Just as he was careful in the opening scene to accommodate the photographer and local politicians, Brady recognizes the value of the reporters and press coverage and knows how to use them to help himself and his cause. The playwrights are careful, though, to keep Brady from appearing as a bitter, irrational Fundamentalist leader. Given the opportunity to lash out verbally at his opponent Henry Drummond through the press, Brady shows "no personal animosity" towards him. Unlike many of the townspeople, Matthew Harrison Brady can view the trial from a greater distance and can see that he, Henry Drummond, and Bert Cates are merely filling roles that had eventually to be played; thus personal feelings are, or should be, set aside.

The brief skirmish between Brady and Hornbeck reinforces the impression made by Brady in the previous dialogue with the reporters and informs the reader that, as they had expected, Hornbeck has been publicly criticizing the Great Commoner. But Brady remains calm, controlled, and confident. The entrance of Brown and Mrs. Brady concludes their conversation and carries the action of the play towards the approaching prayer meeting. Once again, Mrs. Brady is used to foreshadow Brady's eventual collapse with her concern for his health, but the Reverend Brown gradually begins to draw the attention of the theatre audience.

From the beginning of the action, Brown has been overconcerned with impressing Brady with his townspeople and their religious fervor, and his nervousness is apparent as his "show" is about to start. The townspeople enter singing "Revive Us Again" - carefully selected by Lawrence and Lee to indicate their attitude, and quite effective - and wait expectantly before their spiritual leader. Stage directions subtly emphasize the conflict: Brown, backed by Brady, stands before the crowd, while Hornbeck and Drummond stand at opposite fringes. As Brown directs, the crowd imitates with mindless emotions. Yet Lawrence and Lee achieve more than a characterization of the Reverend Brown and the townspeople in the first half of the prayer meeting, for they also employ it as a dramatic device of **exposition**. Howard Blair and Bert Cates had reviewed the theory of evolution for the audience, and now Reverend Brown narrates the Biblical theory of creation for them. At this point its importance may not be apparent, but the confrontation between Brady and Drummond in the next scene will depend upon it.

In contrast to the benign Matthew Harrison Brady, the Reverend Brown is swept up in his own emotional fervor. But when he attacks his daughter and Bert Cates, the townspeople and Brady recoil in shock at the blatant barrage he casts upon the two young people. Yet Lawrence and Lee have designed the scene in such a way that when Brown's emotions overcome his reason, Matthew Harrison Brady steps forward. Literally and symbolically, Brady replaces Brown as the townspeople's leader, much to their gratitude. In place of curses, Brady calls upon the people to forgive one another. He quotes to them from the Bible: "He that troubleth his own house...shall inherit the wind," and explains that "...it is possible to be overzealous to destroy that which you hope to save - so that nothing is left but emptiness." In present context, the quotation is highly appropriate to the Reverend Brown, who symbolizes extreme Fundamentalism, in contrast to Brady, who takes a slightly more enlightened view (and to some more avid believers, as will later appear in the trial, a more liberal view), but in typical Lawrence and Lee fashion the quote will eventually and ironically return to haunt Brady.

In their fine attention to detail, the playwrights direct the townspeople to leave the prayer meeting singing "Go Tell It on the Mountain," which reflects their mellow tone and faith in the word of Matthew Harrison Brady - which they are now ready to defend and spread. Their faith and trust are now wholly invested in Brady, and, as will become evident later, Lawrence and Lee have prepared the audience for the approaching showdown between him and Drummond.

Stage directions indicate that Brady and Drummond are left alone on the scene after the crowd has dispersed. In a sense, Brady is riding the crest of his popularity, even though it is not the Chautauqua style he is accustomed to. The scene and the evening have been entirely his, but as they did before with Hornbeck, the playwrights provide a foil, a contrast, to complicate the reactions of the audience and force them to formulate their own opinions. Brady overwhelms himself with his benevolence, yet he is sincere in his attempt to seek out the cause of the dissolution of their friendship (a fact which in itself deepens the conflict and heightens the interest in their battle). Henry Drummond, however, is not awed by all that he has seen that evening and, following the advice he later gives to Cates, he confronts Brady with the truth-people are constantly changing, and those who do not change with them will be left behind, as Brady has. The impact his words have upon Brady is evidenced by the great orator's stunned, silent retreat. Once again, his quest for truth leaves Henry Drummond standing alone.

Scene Two

Howard and Rachel on the Stand. After the prayer meeting, Lawrence and Lee return their audience to the trial proceedings on the courthouse lawn for the most dramatic scene in the play. Two days have elapsed since the jury selection was completed, thus permitting the playwrights to condense the action on the stage. The curtain rises in the midst of Howard's testimony and implies that preliminary - and less exciting - testimony has already been given. The path to the **climax** of the play is now short and clear.

Howard's appearance in the court is in marked contrast to his opening scene, for his overalls have been replaced by his Sunday suit. The heat persists and it quickly becomes evident that Howard, almost like Bert Cates, is an innocent victim of the evolution controversy. Brady's examination of the young prosecution witness is yet another example of carefully concealed **exposition**, for it presents a more detailed account of the theory of evolution which, to many people - in the gallery, conflicts with the Biblical version reiterated by Brown in the previous scene. Brady's confidence is as obvious as his courtroom tactics. He derides the theory of evolution and makes it the butt of his jokes, including the line about "good American monkeys." Yet the townspeople do not seem to notice the lack of reasoning in his presentation; they show their resentment when Drummond, in an attempt to break Brady's rising rhythm, interrupts his "speech." The move also reveals Drummond's concern for the case Brady is building against his client, and the effect it is having on the jury, the judge, and the townspeople. Brady's speech-emotional and effective-summarizes the prosecution's case and emphasizes the impact that the trial is having on the entire world, and, for the first time, the possibility that Cates will suffer "the full penalty of the law." Both work to maintain interest and build suspense around the approaching outcome of the trial.

In contrast to Brady's serious appeal to the judge, jurors, and spectators, Drummond attempts to treat the conflict between evolution and Fundamentalism lightly, but it is also clear from his first attempts at humor that the townspeople are firmly behind Matthew Harrison Brady. Yet Drummond continues to adapt his language to theirs in hopes of persuading them to listen and to believe what he says. In the midst of Drummond's cross-examination of Howard Blair, the central question of the trial clearly emerges for the first time: Exactly who, or what, is on trial - Bert Cates, the right to think, the anti-evolution law, or all three? For the time being, Lawrence and Lee leave the question unanswered in the audience's mind.

The examination and subsequent cross-examination by Brady and Drummond reveal parallel tactical structures: both lawyers build from factual, informative questions to a final, extensive personal statement. Drummond jeopardizes his client's case when he explains to Brady, the jury, and the spectators that Right, which is determined by the members of a society, is of less importance to him than the one thing which can supply mankind with a direction to follow - Truth. Suddenly, too, the audience can see that Henry Drummond can equal and surpass Brady's eloquence and **diction**. His first convert, Howard Blair, reveals to everyone, including the theatre audience and the spectators that Drummond's tactics are beginning to show results.

The testimony of Brady's final witness, Rachel Brown, was foreshadowed by their conversation at the picnic and by her confession to Cates that she had confided in him. Lawrence and Lee, though, withheld from the audience the context of their conversation until now in order to maintain suspense. Her fear and confusion, coupled with Bert's betrayed and defeated attitude, combine to prepare the audience for her damaging testimony. Drummond's frequent interruptions during her examination, in a futile attempt to delay her testimony and break his rhythm, increase the tension and suspense. Her story of Bert's break with the church over her father's handling of the funeral services for the boy who drowned sharpens the conflict between Cates and Brown and helps illustrate the pressure which Rachel is, and has been, under.

This pressure, combined with the overbearance of the judge, Brady, and the townspeople, destroys Rachel's composure, but not before Brady is able to use her to reveal some of the statements made by Bert Cates about God and marriage. In addition to seriously jeopardizing the defense case, her testimony enables the playwrights to reveal more of Cates' character through his concern for her safety. After her disclosures and departure, Drummond finds himself and his client facing a jury and gallery of spectators convinced that Bert Cates is guilty.

Brady Versus Drummond. Although Brady's case for the prosecution had severely damaged Cates' chances for acquittal, Drummond has not yet called any witnesses. When the judge, however, upholds each of Brady's objections to the scientists Drummond called to testify, it suddenly appears that Brady had won. Drummond's defense of his witnesses reemphasizes a statement made earlier by Bert Cates to Rachel - that evolution and the Bible are not necessarily in conflict. But his plan to educate the spectators and the jurors is thwarted by the judge's refusal to let him put the law on trial. The suspense builds with each attempt Drummond makes to find a scientist acceptable to Brady and with the gradual realization that the defense lawyer will be stripped of each of his witnesses. The playwrights effectively focus the attention on Drummond, who appears to have been beaten by Matthew Harrison Brady and the forces of Fundamentalism. The testimony is complete, the defense is stymied, and the jury and townspeople are clearly lined up in support of Brady, his defense of Fundamentalism, and the anti-evolution law.

Lawrence and Lee effectively employ the element of surprise by having Drummond, in a final, desperate attempt to salvage a portion of victory, call Brady to the stand to testify as an expert on the Bible. All of the action in the play thus far has been designed to lead to this confrontation between the two giants, and the opportunity is given Brady to shun it. But his pride, his overconfidence, and his desire for a complete victory over not only Bert Cates but also Henry Drummond as well clouds his legal judgment (if he had declined, the trial would have been over) and the advice of his astute associate Tom Davenport, who has accurately assessed Drummond's ability. The numerous "Amens" from the spectators clearly indicate who their favorite is.

With his first few questions Drummond establishes before the court that the Biblical expert has not read any books written by Charles Darwin; he then suddenly stuns the Great Commoner and the court by demanding of Brady an explanation of how he could then accuse the evolutionist's works of conflicting with the Bible. Brady is confused and must ask to have the question repeated. The laughter from the spectators indicates that Drummond has scored. Davenport evens the score for the prosecution, though, when he objects to Drummond's sly attempt to read from the *Origin of Species,* and the crowd applauds.

Both sides having "drawn blood," Drummond turns his attention to the Bible; yet before taking their two characters into the battle, the playwrights establish for the audience the basic tenet of Fundamentalism that will be the key to the forthcoming testimony - the literal interpretation of the Bible as the Word of God.

In the first few minutes of his examination of Brady, Drummond questions him on four interpretations of Bible passages: (1) the swallowing of Jonah by the "great fish,"

(2) Joshua stopping the sun, (3) the creation of Cain's wife, and (4) sex and the "holy people" of the Old Testament. The questioning concerning Jonah was designed to test Brady's literal interpretation of the three days spent by Jonah in the great fish's belly. Although Brady thwarts Drummond's motive by stating that God could make it possible (which was followed by loud "Amens," a reminder and reflection of the townspeople's feelings), a minor incident serves as a clue to the agnostic's knowledge of the Bible: when Drummond refers to the whale, Brady condescendingly corrects him; but Drummond quickly corrects Brady by pointing out that the actual wording is "great fish." Although Brady does not seem to notice, the audience can sense that Drummond may know the Bible better than Brady.

In an attempt to minimize the miracle of Joshua stopping the sun in order that the Israelites might defeat their enemies, Drummond asks if Houdini could do the same. Brady falls back on his insurmountable premise that God controls the universe and can make and change natural law as He pleases, but his answer does not evoke any "Amens" from the spectators, for he cannot reconcile the Biblical belief that the sun revolved around the earth with Copernicus and the later discovery of the workings of the solar system.

Drummond increases the tempo of his questions as he turns to the unexplained creation of Cain's wife, and Brady offers no answer to the Biblical riddle. Yet without answers Drummond cannot build; after criticizing Brady for his noticeable lack of curiosity, he moves to a more shocking line of questioning in order to evoke some answers - sex and the holy people. But again, Brady has no answer.

Although none of his questions have directly touched upon the theory of evolution and its relationship to the Biblical version of creation, Drummond has worked to raise in the minds of the jurors and spectators questions left unanswered by a purely literal translation of the Bible.

Davenport's objection appears to have stopped Drummond's questions, but Lawrence and Lee use it to lead to the next level in the rising action. Drummond's lengthy speech to the spectators on the "individual human mind" and its relationship to progress is one of the play's most effective passages. Disregarding the rhetoric of the eloquent, Drummond turns to the Hillsboro jury and speaks of progress and the price man must pay for it:

Darwin moved us forward to a hilltop, where he could look back and see the way from which we came. But for this view, this insight, this knowledge, we must abandon our faith in the pleasant poetry of Genesis.

Brady's reply cannot negate Drummond's persuasiveness, especially when countered with the reminder that God granted man the ability to think - and man, not God, is attempting to restrict it. Lawrence and Lee employ the "sponge" dialogue to show two things: first, that Drummond is in complete control of Brady, and, second, that the townspeople are beginning to lose faith in Brady. The applause from the scientists at Drummond's roaring line - "This man wishes to be accorded the same privilege as a sponge. He wishes to think" - marks the first open support of the defense lawyer. At this point Drummond, as well as Brady, is aware of the changing mood of the spectators, and he begins to close in on his prey.

The conflict between literal interpretation of the Bible and science is Drummond's next target, for he knows that, according to the Bible, the earth was created in the year 4004 B.C. (as calculated by Bishop Usher), but the geologist Dr. Paige has a rock estimated to be over ten million years old. Brought into the open, Drummond uses the conflict as a trap to ensnare Brady. He first ridicules his precise dating of the creation, and then challenges the Fundamentalist premise that the creation of the heavens, the earth, and all of the living things upon it, including man, occurred in seven twenty-four-hour days - for according to that same book the sun, which is used to measure the length of the day, was not created until the fourth day. The suspense builds as Brady evades the central question: Was the first day a twenty-four-hour day? The Fundamentalist leader flounders, for he knows that his followers firmly believe that it was, but Drummond's questions have positioned him in such a way that to adhere to the twenty-four-hour day before the creation of the sun would make him appear ridiculous to everyone else.

When he finally admits that it could have been longer, the trap is sprung. Brady cannot turn back, and the turning point of the action - that is, the most significant dramatic situation in the play, the moment in which the action takes a definite turn towards the **climax** - has occurred, and from this point on Lawrence and Lee build to the **climax**. Drummond turns from his attack of the Fundamentalist belief in a literal interpretation of the Bible to Brady himself.

As he ridicules before his followers Brady's tragic flaw, his vanity, the laughter builds and Drummond seeks to reveal to the spectators the true Matthew Harrison Brady. He climaxes his attack and the play with his final question, "Must men go to prison because they are at odds with the self-appointed prophet?"

Dramatically, Drummond dismisses Brady before he can plead with the crowd that has by now deserted him. The spectators exit - this time with Drummond-leaving the broken

Brady alone with his wife. Lawrence and Lee end the most dramatic scene of the play not with the audience hating Brady, but with them sympathizing with a man who has been left "standing still."

ACT THREE

After the turning point and the **climax** of the play (which occur either late in the second act of a three-act play or in the third act), the playwrights must begin to construct the resolution in which they gather loose ends of the plot together, dispose of characters, and, in general, bring the audience back into their own world. Finally, the **denouement**, or ending of the play, will give the audience members a glimpse or indication of the new situation surrounding the characters as they leave the stage for the final time.

Scene One

The Verdict. The setting for the third and final act of *Inherit the Wind* is once again the courthouse lawn. The lighting directions - "low and somber" - set the mood. Only the three major figures, Cates, Drummond, and Brady, occupy the stage, and their actions, or lack of actions, prepare the audience for the finale: Drummond is, as usual, relaxed, "meditative"; Cates is weary, exhausted, as he is unaccustomed to the furor that has enveloped him; and Brady eats - another subtle characterization and foreshadowing.

Hornbeck's entrance shatters the silence, supplies the audience with vital information, and sets the action of the act in motion. His sarcastic soliloquy (the term being used loosely, for although he is not alone on stage, none of the three others listens to him) informs the audience that the testimony has been completed and the jury has retired to "wrestle with justice."

The element of suspense that Lawrence and Lee build in the setting of the third act and increase slightly in Hornbeck's **exposition**, intensifies in the dialogue between Cates and Drummond. The mention of prison, and Drummond's acknowledgment of that possibility, adds another complication, for although it has appeared evident throughout the trial that Cates would be found guilty, never before has the likelihood of a jail sentence been raised. Drummond's analogy of the trial to a fire reveals his insight to the Hillsboro people and takes on added significance later when the mayor suggests that the judge "go easy" on Cates. Drummond's evasiveness when asked by Cates if he thinks the jury will find him guilty seems to confirm the audience's anticipations, and imperceptibly the suspense has been shifted from the verdict to the ensuing sentence.

The Chicago lawyer's "Golden Dancer" speech takes the audience into the mind and memory of the man so many people have watched and known, but few know well. More important, though, it serves as the outlet of one of the play's most important ideas central to the purpose of the play - the quest for Truth, and the revelation of anything or person who pretends to be something other than what he really is: "And if it's a lie-show it up for what it really is!"

The presence of the radio man in the play is historically accurate, yet he serves a larger purpose. Progress is a key **theme** in the play, especially in its relationship to Brady and the people of Hillsboro, and the radio serves as its symbol in *Inherit the Wind*. Drummond's conversation with the radio operator supplies the third act with its only humor-comic relief at the expense of the radio man in the midst of the tension surrounding the wait for the verdict. Brady's meeting with the symbol of progress evokes a feeling of sympathy for the once-great orator. His booming voice, trained to travel across a sea of faces without artificial amplification, cannot adjust to the enunciator, but Brady himself immediately assesses the value of such an apparatus in carrying his words beyond the boundaries of the town square. His language immediately attempts to portray his "intellectuality" - and in the attempt he appears as little more than an educated fool.

Drummond's earlier analogy and his comment "a lot of people's shoes are getting hot" become painfully relevant during the mayor's conversation with the judge. The speech serves as an indication of the effect that Drummond and the trial have had upon the legislators who created the anti-evolution law. Suddenly elections in November become more important than justice in July.

Stage directions bring the audience's attention back to the approaching verdict from the previous action (which allowed for a plausible passage of time for the jury to continue with its deliberations); Hornbeck's shift, a change in lighting, and the shout from offstage simultaneously sharpen the tension. Rachel's absence adds yet another unanswered question to the audience's mind. The intensity and action build with the radio announcer's emotional narrative and are climaxed by a moment of still silence as the single slip of paper is passed from Sillers to Meeker to the judge. The verdict comes as no surprise, but the mixed reaction from the spectators reflects the effect that Drummond's evolution lesson had on the townspeople. Brady's victory seems tainted.

Yet the moment of suspense has not passed. The playwrights use the radio announcer to restate the jury's verdict and to prepare the audience for the approaching sentence. The uproar following the reading of the verdict confuses the judge, and Drummond interrupts just as he is about to pass sentence, thus sustaining the suspense even more. In contrast to the pandemonium surrounding him, Bert Cates remains the Shy, mild, yet highly principled, country schoolteacher. Mrs. Blair's retort provides the first real effect of the guilty verdict, and in a sense, the first sentence. But the scientists' applause following Cates' remarks reveals that the spectators are not unanimous supporters of the verdict.

At the moment of sentencing the theatre audience is aware, although Brady is not, of the mayor's conversation with the judge. This use of dramatic **irony** enables the playwrights to shift the audience's attention from the judge to Brady, whom they can now expect to react violently to what will most likely be a small fine. The insignificance of the punishment marks Brady's second setback in two days, yet more are to come. Drummond's agile legal mind prevents him from using the court to propound his views expressed in a prepared statement and further frustrates the great orator. The descent of the "hawkers" reinforces the idea that many of the townspeople used the trial for monetary gain, and Howard's remark to Melinda reflects the confusion that Drummond, the verdict, and the sentence have thrown the spectators into. Hornbeck's discussion with Meeker, unheard by the audience, helps sustain interest now that the sentence has been passed, as does Rachel's absence.

Brady's pathetic attempt to gain the attention of the spectators after court has been adjourned provides the play with tragic humor and prepares the audience for his collapse. He fails to realize that his one-time followers have lost interest in additional rhetoric. As spectators slip away, Brady grows desperate, but the final indignity comes when his speech is preempted by "Matinee Musical." His collapse and removal - part of the play's resolution - signify not only his defeat at the hands of Drummond and his rejection by the people of Hillsboro, but the defeat of Fundamentalism as well. The spontaneous outpouring of undelivered inauguration speeches evokes a final feeling of sympathy for the fallen "also-ran." Drummond and Cates openly show sympathy for Brady, and the play-wrights effectively elicit a similar response from the audience by way of Hornbeck's bitter sarcasm, which indirectly compels the audience to come to Brady's defense.

The playwrights vocalize the obvious question in the minds of the spectators and audience through Cates' query of whether he had won or lost. Drummond's explanation of whom the real jury was and what effect the trial had levied on the anti-evolution law forms the transition into his next speech and the key **theme** of the play - the role each individual plays in the battle for Truth and Freedom. The playwrights quickly go to work to gather the loose ends of the plot and dispose of the characters. Since Hornbeck fixed bail, Cates is free to go, pending the appeal of his case. Rachel's entrance and her announcement of her decision to leave her father completes the play's subplot and reinforces the **theme** central to the play - the right, and necessity, to think.

It must be said, however, that Rachel's absence during the most important part of the trial and her happy disposition upon entering the courtyard arena threaten the plausibility of the plot. The play-wrights' attempt to justify her decision to leave Hillsboro with her reading of the *Origin of Species* (quite a task for less than a day's time), but her sudden disregard for Cates' fate - it was only as an afterthought that she' invited him to leave with her - is disconcerting.

Lawrence and Lee contrast in the closing moments of the play the two characters yet to be disposed of. Drummond emerges as the defender of Brady's right to think, even though minutes earlier the two had fought on opposite sides. The transition is more than Hornbeck, the natural cynic, can accept, and provides him with his exit to write a story about the atheist "who believes in God." Rachel and Bert's exit leaves Henry Drummond alone once more, and his symbolic act of slapping the Bible and the *Origin of Species* together reinforces the belief that when viewed with open minds, science and religion can both safely exist.

THE SCOPES MONKEY TRIAL

. . . .

INTRODUCTION

In the summer of 1925, as American prosperity under President Calvin Coolidge attempted to erase bitter memories of World War I, the attention of the American people and of much of the world was drawn to a sleepy Tennessee town where a schoolteacher by the name of John T. Scopes had volunteered to test the newly enacted Butler Act, a law which forbade the teaching of evolution in the state's public schools. For Jerome Lawrence and Robert E. Lee the trial served as the genesis of *Inherit the Wind*. It is hoped that an understanding of the events which preceded the trial, of the major participants who gathered at Dayton, and of the trial itself will aid the student in his appreciation of the play, his knowledge of this particular period in American history, and his role as an individual in a society where the freedom of speech can never be taken for granted.

The text of the Butler Act follows:

The Butler Act

An Act prohibiting the teaching of the Evolution Theory in all the Universities, Normals and all other public schools of Tennessee, which are supported

in whole or in part by the public school funds of the State, and to provide penalties for the violation thereof.

Section 1. Be It Enacted By The General Assembly Of The State Of Tennessee, That it shall be unlawful for any teacher in any of the Universities, Normals and all other public schools of the state which are supported in whole or in part by the public school funds of the State, to teach any theory that denies the story of the Divine Creation of man as taught in the Bible, and to teach instead that man has descended from a lower order of animals.

Bible, and to teach instead that man has descended from a lower order of animals.

Section 2. Be It Further Enacted, That any teacher found guilty of the violation of this Act, shall be guilty of a misdemeanor and upon conviction, shall be fined not less than One Hundred ($100.00) Dollars nor more than Five Hundred ($500.00) Dollars for each offense.

Section 3. Be It Further Enacted, That this Act take effect from and after its passage, the public welfare requiring it.

FUNDAMENTALISM

As soon as it became evident, first in England and then later in America, that Darwin's theory of evolution by natural selection was a plausible alternative to the creation theory as set forth in Genesis, the battle lines between science and religion were drawn. Up until that time the two had lived in peaceful coexistence, interrupted only at times when men such as Galileo and Copernicus had dared to challenge traditional "scientific" assumptions based upon the Bible; but after Darwin and *Origin of Species,* the two would find it difficult to ever agree again.

Prior to *Origin of Species,* the vast majority of Christians in Europe and America readily accepted a literal interpretation of the Bible. But as the number of supporters of the theory of evolution increased and were multiplied by historical scholarship and Biblical criticism in the late 1800s that cast doubt upon the total reliability of the Bible, many of the believers of the fundamentals of "the Word of God" began to waver in their beliefs.

In 1895 a group of conservative Protestants met and drew up a set of doctrines which later became known as the famous *Five Points. The Five Points* crystalized tenets of Fundamentalism as they proclaimed their belief in:

1. the infallibility of the Bible

2. the virgin birth of Jesus Christ

3. the divinity of Jesus Christ

4. the substitute atonement of Jesus Christ

5. the physical resurrection of Jesus Christ and his eventual Second Coming

In the year 1922 the Fundamentalists, under the leadership of William Jennings Bryan, attempted to persuade the legislators of the state of Kentucky to pass the nation's first anti-evolution law. The Fundamentalists had hoped to make it illegal for a teacher to teach the theory of evolution in any public school within the state, but teachers, educators, and scientists in Kentucky organized their supporters and applied opposite pressure on the lawmakers. As a result of their efforts, the anti-evolution bill fell one vote short of passage. The Fundamentalists, however, were not easily discouraged and in the next two years anti-evolution bills similar to the one placed before the legislators in Kentucky were introduced in seven other states. None, though, became law.

In the same year that the Kentucky lawmakers rejected their anti-evolution bill, John Washington Butler was elected to Tennessee's House of Representatives as a professed anti-evolutionist. After reading Darwin's *Origin of Species*, Butler sat down and drafted a bill which was designed to prohibit the teaching of evolution in the public schools in Tennessee.

His proposal was passed by the Tennessee House of Representatives and Senate and signed into law by the governor.

Forty-six days later, John Thomas Scopes was arrested for violation of the Butler Anti-Evolution Act. Within the week William Jennings Bryan, the Fundamentalist leader who had greatly influenced the Tennessee legislators, volunteered to travel to Dayton to help prosecute Scopes, and the showdown between the Fundamentalists and the evolutionists appeared imminent.

WILLIAM JENNINGS BRYAN

Prior to his entrance onto the stage at Dayton, William Jennings Bryan had established himself as a perennial presidential candidate and a leader of the Fundamentalist movement. A three-time candidate in the presidential political arena and a three-time loser, Bryan had turned his attention in the twenties to the campaign to defeat evolution, and the trail led to Dayton.

William Jennings Bryan's life was chiefly an interaction of two forces: religion and politics. For both, and his beliefs in both, he was himself a strict fundamental believer in the Bible and an influential Illinois politician.

Bryan was born on March 19, 1860 in Illinois. In 1883 Bryan was admitted to the Illinois Bar and set up a practice in Jacksonville that same year. Following four disappointing years of practice in Illinois, the Bryans moved to Lincoln, Nebraska, where his success as a lawyer remained only moderate. Although the area was a strong Republican stronghold and Bryan, like his father, was a dedicated Democrat, he quickly immersed himself in the Democratic organization in Lincoln and soon was spending more time as politician than as lawyer. To help supplement her husband's shrinking income, Bryan's wife, Mary, decided to renew her studies and pass her Bar exam.

Bryan's frequent and eloquent orations in support of various local candidates helped spread his name and build his reputation to the point where, in 1890, he was approached by the leaders of the local Democratic party and asked to serve as a candidate for the state legislature. Since the voters of the area had long been Republican by tradition, Bryan was considered by most observers as no more than a political sacrifice. In typical Bryan fashion, though, the young lawyer marched into the fray full of confidence and vigor, and challenged his Republican opponent to a series of debates. The Republican underestimated Bryan's ability at the speaker's stand, and, after the debates, was upset by the young lawyer from Illinois.

His father's political connections earned Bryan a place on the prestigious Ways and Means Committee in the state capital, but an impressive and emotional anti-tariff speech before the members of the Nebraska legislature quickly earned Bryan the reputation as a politician in his own right. Bryan sided with the farmer and the small businessman, who felt that they were being forced to suffer at the hands of Eastern businessmen and the tariffs designed to protect American industry, for these prevented the unlimited importation of cheaper goods from foreign countries.

In addition to attacking the barons of Wall Street on the tariff issue, Bryan soon began advocating the coinage of both gold and silver at the ratio of 16 to 1. At that time gold was, as it had been for years, the only acceptable monetary standard. But the demand for gold exceeded the available supply, and the price was constantly rising. Silver was more plentiful than gold in the West and the settlers believed that if silver, along with gold, was made into dollars, money would be more plentiful and they could quickly repay their loans. In reality, the situation was more complex than either the farmers or Bryan realized, for the money standard of the United States affected the world, and vice versa. But Bryan quickly emerged as the leader of the free-silver advocates with promises of economic recovery if the United States would adopt a bimetal standard of currency. His stand on silver enabled him to gain re-election in 1892, although he was never aware of the complexities, both foreign and domestic, of the silver issue and the flaws in his logic.

The recession of 1883 increased the belief of many people in the West that the gold standard was the root of the farmers' and the country's economic problems, and Bryan, as the free-silver spokesman, was nominated as the Democratic candidate for the position of United States Senator from the state of Nebraska. Even though he captured over seventy-five percent of the popular vote, he was defeated, for at that time Senators were elected by state legislatures - and Nebraska was still solidly Republican. This obvious violation of the people's right to elect their representatives inspired Bryan to campaign for the direct election of Senators until it became the Seventeenth Amendment in 1913.

Nominated For Presidency. Bryan traveled to Chicago as a Nebraska delegate to the Democratic National **Convention** in 1896. Unknown to anyone, the young orator already had visions of himself as the next Democratic candidate for the office of President. As the **convention** opened and the delegates began the clumsy process of choosing from as many as half a dozen possible candidates one man to keep their party in the White House, Bryan quietly waited for the opportunity to present himself. When, after the delegates had been deadlocked on the first four ballots, the thirty-six-year-old Nebraskan delegate rose to speak, no one imagined that they were about to hear what has been called the "most famous convention speech in American history." William Jennings Bryan, with a "voice like an organ," swept the delegates to their feet with his now-famous "Cross of Gold" speech:

> **We will answer their demand for a gold standard by saying to them: You shall not press down upon the brow of labor this crown of thorns; you shall not crucify mankind on a cross of gold.**

The Boy Orator was nominated on the next ballot as the emotional delegates forgot about the other candidates in their enthusiasm to name William Jennings Bryan as their candidate for the presidency.

Backed by big business and Wall Street, the Republican party poured more than sixteen million dollars into the campaign of Bryan's opponent, William McKinley. The Democrats, though, spent only slightly more than four hundred thousand dollars on Bryan's campaign, yet Bryan lost only by a margin of less than six hundred thousand votes. Bryan had done a respectable job, but he was outnumbered and outbid by the barons of Wall Street.

Bryan lost to McKinley again in 1900, and the Democratic nomination in 1904 went to conservative Alton Parker, who was defeated by Republican Theodore Roosevelt. In 1908, Bryan was once again the also-ran and William Howard Taft was the new president. Bryan hoped to be called by his party in 1912, but when Woodrow Wilson was nominated, he came out in his support. Bryan campaigned heartily for Wilson and was rewarded with the post of Secretary of State - the highest appointive position in the government. Bryan immediately set out to fill the government with as many of the persons who had supported him in his three unsuccessful bids for the presidency as possible. As his appointments reached ludicrous proportions, criticism, especially from the Eastern newspapers, rained down upon him and Wilson. Bryan made matters worse by securing permission from the President to continue on the Chautauqua circuit. The idea of the Secretary of State lecturing to a tent full of people often in an atmosphere of subtle and not so subtle overtones of religion shocked and offended many people.

Campaign Against Evolution. Bryan eventually resigned his post as Secretary of State when Wilson ignored his advice that the U.S. **refrain** from becoming involved in World War I. This marked the unofficial end of Bryan's political career. His departure from politics left him prepared to direct all his energies towards the battle against the evolutionists. In his travels he spoke out against science and evolution, saying "It is better to trust the Rock of Ages, than to know the age of rocks."

Bryan turned to the legislatures of the states of Kentucky, West Virginia, Florida, and Georgia with his appeals for the passage of anti-evolution laws. Although he pushed for the passage of many anti-evolution laws, Bryan was opposed to the attachment of any penalty for the crime. He argued that the existence of the law would be reason enough for the teachers in the state to not teach evolution, and he feared that opponents of the bill would use the penalty provision as a weapon to defeat the bill. Nevertheless, the Tennessee legislature passed the Butler Act as it had originally been written with a fine of one to five hundred dollars. Inspired by the passage of the country's first anti-evolution law, Bryan continued to travel and lecture on the evil of evolution in the spring of 1925.

CLARENCE DARROW

Clarence Seward Darrow was born on April 18, 1857, in the small town of Kinsman, Ohio. Clarence disliked all of his school experience, including a year of college, and became the schoolteacher at Vernon, a town three miles from Kinsman. There he abolished corporal punishment and lengthened the recess to allow more time for baseball. He realized, though, that he could not enjoy teaching as a career and began studying law.

After a year in a Youngstown law office, Darrow took and passed his Bar exam, became a lawyer, and moved to Andover, Ohio. By the time he was thirty he had established himself as a fair country lawyer. But Clarence Darrow yearned for more than cases involving horse collars and boundary lines, so in 1887 he moved his family to Chicago.

Away from his friends and his local reputation, Darrow barely survived his first two years in Chicago as a lawyer, but he met many new friends with whom he exchanged ideas and shared experiences. His friendship with a future governor of Illinois, John P. Altgeld, helped lead him to a position as a lawyer for the city of Chicago. In two years he quickly worked his way up the ranks of lawyers working for the city until 1893, when he was offered a lucrative position as a lawyer for the Chicago and Northwestern Railway. Against his better judgment he accepted it, but a year later he resigned to defend Eugene V. Debs, the leader of the Pullman Strike that almost crippled the railroad for whom Darrow had worked. In 1895 the case went to court, but the charges were dismissed on a technicality when the prosecution realized that it could not defeat Clarence Darrow. Although Debs was later given a minor sentence for a lesser charge, Clarence Darrow had begun to establish a reputation in the eyes of the public as a defender of the underprivileged.

Darrow Meets Bryan. In 1896 John P. Altgeld and others persuaded Darrow to be a candidate for United States Senator from Illinois. At the Democratic **convention** in Chicago Darrow met for the first time the Boy Orator from the Platte - William Jennings Bryan. Although not intended to be a candidate, Bryan swept the delegates into his camp with an emotional speech that captured the nomination. Darrow, though never sure if he really wanted to become a politician, campaigned throughout the state, but was defeated by a margin of one hundred votes.

He returned to his law practice in Chicago, secretly relieved that he had not been elected, but six years later, in 1902, he was once again talked into running for a seat in the Illinois legislature. Although he was victorious, he was delayed in taking his seat in the state capital, for he was asked by the United Mine Workers Association to defend their president,

John Mitchell, who had led a strike to protect miners' wages and workers' conditions.

Darrow spent many years arguing cases for labor unions and acting as defense in difficult criminal cases. Darrow attempted to retire from law, but the Scopes Trial was to bring him out of retirement at the age of sixty-eight. Two years earlier, in the summer of 1923, Darrow had responded to a letter attacking science that William Jennings Bryan had written to the editor of the Chicago Tribune. Darrow, in the interest of "reaching the truth," posed fifty questions concerning the Bible and Fundamentalism to Bryan, but the anti-evolution leader refused to answer the questions. Two years later however, in the town of Dayton, Tennessee, Darrow would again ask the questions and this time Bryan would reply.

THE BIRTH OF THE TRIAL

In May 1925, the Chattanooga News carried the following announcement:

A legal test of the Tennessee law prohibiting the teaching of evolution in public schools and colleges is being sought by the American Civil Liberties Union, a national free speech organization, according to Prof. Clarence R. Skinner of Tufts College, chairman of the Union's committee on academic freedom. Prof. Skinner states that "the law strikes so serious a blow at scientific teaching that we cannot let the issue rest until it has been passed upon by the highest courts."

"We are looking for a Tennessee teacher who is willing to accept our services in testing this law in the courts," Prof. Skinner states. "Our lawyers think a friendly test case can be arranged without costing a teacher his or her job. Distinguished counsel have volunteered their services. All we need now is a willing client. By this test we hope to render a real service to freedom of teaching throughout the country, for we do not believe the law will be sustained."

Thirty-eight miles away in the sleepy town of Dayton, George W. Rappelyea, an outspoken evolutionist, read the ACLU proposal and stopped to consider the possibilities. A trial designed to test the nation's first anti-evolution law guaranteed the participants an enormous amount of publicity - state and national as well as local, and, in Rappelyea's mind, more business for the town's merchants.

Rappelyea hurried to Robinson's Drug Store, the town's unofficial meeting place, where he immediately struck up an argument over the constitutionality of the Butler Act with Walter White, superintendent of the Rhea County schools, and Sue Hicks, a young lawyer. Although neither of these two men could be called avid Fundamentalists, both supported the legislature's right to pass laws governing the curriculum of the state's public schools.

As White and Hicks sipped their Cokes, Rappelyea produced a copy of the Chattanooga News and proposed that Dayton be the site of a trial that would rule on the constitutionality of the Butler Act. The lawyer Hicks, who perhaps began to envision the role he might play in a test case, soon agreed that the trial would certainly bolster the town's business, and the skeptical White was finally convinced that the trial might be the best thing ever to happen to Dayton. All that remained was for them to find a willing volunteer.

The most obvious candidate to fill the role of defendant was the local high-school biology teacher, who, in addition to his teaching duties, was also the principal. The risk, however, was too great for a man with family responsibilities. A second and better choice turned out to be John Thomas Scopes, the young, unmarried, first-year science teacher and football coach from Illinois. Scopes had substituted for the regular biology teacher during the last two weeks of the school year and thus had become eligible to serve as the sacrifice. The school year had ended for Dayton Central High School on the first day of May, but Scopes had delayed returning North because he had recently met a young, pretty blonde whom he wanted to take to a church social.

Scopes refrained from entering the controversy at first, but, when asked, explicitly stated that it was impossible to teach biology without teaching evolution. To prove his point he took from a nearby shelf a copy of Hunter's *Civic Biology*, the official textbook selected by the Tennessee Textbook Commission for use in public-school biology classes. Scopes flipped through the book until he stopped at page 194, where Hunter explained the theory of evolution as "the belief that simple forms of life on the earth slowly and gradually gave rise to those more complex, and that thus, ultimately, the most complex forms came into existence."

Ironically enough, Hunter's textbook and its now "illegal" explanation of Darwin's theory of evolution had been used in the state since 1909. Ten years later, under the authority of the state legislature, the Textbook Commission had directed the public schools to implement Hunter's *Civic Biology* in their science classrooms. As Arthur Garfield Hays, prominent ACLU attorney, later pointed out, Scopes would have broken the law if he had not used Hunter's *Civic Biology* just as much as he broke the law when he did.

Scopes Volunteers. Scopes confirmed that he had substituted for the ailing biology teacher during the final two weeks of the school term, and he admitted that he had reviewed Hunter's *Civic Biology* in class. To no one's concern, he could not, however, recall precisely which day he had discussed Darwin's theory of evolution with his students, but he agreed to volunteer as the defendant in a test case of the Butler Act.

Rappelyea set the legal machinery in motion with a telegram to the American Civil Liberties Union in New York informing them that Dayton had their willing client.

The ACLU was founded to protect and defend any individual, regardless of race, religion, or political affiliation, whose constitutional rights were believed to have been violated. Shortly after Tennessee's Governor Austin Peay had signed the country's first anti-evolution law, ACLU's founder and director, Roger Baldwin, proposed to prove in the courts that Tennessee's Butler Act violated the First Amendment of the United States Constitution, "Congress shall make no law respecting an established religion, or prohibiting free exercise thereof; or abridging the freedom of speech...."

After the ACLU advertised for a test case and received news from Dayton that John T. Scopes had volunteered, Baldwin wired Rappelyea: "We will cooperate Scopes case with financial help, legal advice and publicity." He announced to the press that the ACLU would "take the Scopes case to the United States Supreme

Court if necessary to establish that a teacher may tell the truth without being thrown in jail."

Rappelyea then signed a complaint which charged that, on April 24, 1925, John T. Scopes had taught a classroom of students in Dayton High School the theory of evolution. Scopes was arrested on May the sixth and charged with violating the recently passed Butler Act. Three judges bound him over to the grand jury; bond was set and paid without Scopes having to spend a single day or night in the Rhea County jail.

Scopes had naively hoped that the trial would not attract much attention nor completely upset his summer plans, but after one of Rappelyea's telegrams to the Chattanooga newspapers had been picked up by a national wire service and flashed across the country, those hopes were shattered. On the thirteenth of May, at the urging of the World Christian Fundamentals Association, William Jennings Bryan announced in Pittsburg that he would offer his services to the state prosecution if he were asked. Unknown to him at that time, Herbert Hicks, a member of the prosecution staff, had already wired a request.

On the following day, May 14, John Randolph Neal announced that he was going to represent the young science teacher as chief counsel for the defense. Neal, along with four other professors, had been dismissed from the University of Tennessee in a controversy over the selection of an evolution textbook. The liberal lawyer had established a private law school soon after his dismissal and it is quite possible that he came to Dayton with hopes that he and the theory of evolution could gain their revenge on the Fundamentalist forces dominating Tennessee. Neal, however, was concerned with more than the legitimacy of the theory of evolution, for he felt that the trial should establish "the freedom of teaching, or what is more important, the freedom of learning."

Enter Mencken. In New York social critic and reporter Henry Louis Mencken, better known as H.L. Mencken, worked to convince two prominent liberal lawyers, Clarence Darrow and Dudley Field Malone, to volunteer their services to Scopes and the ACLU. As a reporter for the Baltimore Morning Herald and the Baltimore Sun, Mencken had first established himself as a book reviewer, but his essays soon turned to criticism - mocking, sarcastic, cynical attacks on American life. Nothing was sacred to Mencken; organized religion, the middle class, and big business all were dissected and derided under his acid-sharp pen. "Nobody gives a damn about that yap schoolteacher," he insisted before Darrow and Malone. "The thing to do is make a fool out of Bryan."

No love was lost between the Fundamentalists and Mencken, who had labeled the Fundamentalist stronghold, the South, as the "Bible Belt" and her inhabitants as "gaping primates" and "yokels." After discussing the Butler Act, the trial, and Bryan with Mencken and Malone, Darrow agreed for the first time in his entire legal career to volunteer his services to a defendant without being asked. He and Malone offered to pay their own expenses and to accept no remittance for their work, for they both were concerned only with preventing Bryan and the Fundamentalists from taking control of the public school system.

Scopes and Neal were pleased to learn of the offer from Darrow, the most famous living criminal lawyer, and Malone, a former Assistant Secretary of State under Bryan and a defender of minority causes; but the American Civil Liberties Union was not. The Board of Directors had planned to staff the defense with a number of their conservative and highly respected constitutional attorneys like Arthur Garfield Hays or Bainbridge Colby, and they prepared to oppose the entrance of the two radical and controversial lawyers Darrow and Malone.

The American Civil Liberties Union was determined to prevent the Scopes trial from becoming a circus and they believed that the courtroom antics of Darrow would jeopardize the case. Malone, however, who had come to the meeting to defend himself and Darrow, pointed out that the prosecution had already taken the first step in turning what should have been a case of constitutional law into a circus when they accepted the services of William Jennings Bryan, even though he had not practiced law for over thirty years. Bryan's entrance could be interpreted only as part of a plan to "put the town on the map" or a means of introducing not another legal counsel to the proceedings, but a Fundamentalist orator. In addition, the townspeople of Dayton had determined that the trial should serve more than the cause of justice, and had begun to prepare to accommodate the hundreds of spectators, reporters, and fanatics who would soon descend upon the quiet little town with money in their pockets.

Finally, after both sides had repeatedly expressed their feelings on the effect Darrow would have on their case, someone thought to ask the defendant whom he would prefer to have present his case. Scopes had already decided that if asked he would request that Clarence Darrow head his defense. The ACLU had little choice but to accept Darrow and Malone, but they added Hays and Colby and insisted that the defense lawyers follow the plan of the ACLU rather than their own.

The first priority of the Union was to move the trial from the circuit court in Dayton to a federal court in one of the state's larger cities. The change of venue would save them a considerable amount of time and money, but it would also assure them of a more sophisticated and educational atmosphere. In addition, the immediate move to a federal court would hasten a judgment on the constitutionality of the law.

What the ACLU directors did not fully realize was that the people of Dayton were, for the most part, more concerned with the effect of the trial on their town than the constitutionality of the law. For example, at the time of Scopes' arrest the grand jury was not scheduled to convene for several weeks, but when word leaked out that persons in nearby Chattanooga were attempting to prepare a test case that would precede the Scopes trial, the local judge, John T. Raulston, immediately announced that a special session of the grand jury would be summoned on May 25. Soon after, the Chattanooga threat dissipated.

While the ACLU and the defense lawyers were preparing to have the Scopes trial moved into a federal court, the legal machinery in Dayton was beginning to turn much faster. Legal jurisdiction of Dayton and Rhea County fell to Eighteenth Judicial Circuit Judge John T. Raulston, a former Methodist preacher whose term was set to expire in 1926. Like the town of Dayton, Judge Raulston needed publicity. Reelection in 1926 would be difficult, but it would be all the more difficult if he lost the support of the people of Dayton. Were Dayton to lose the glory of the first anti-evolution trial, Judge Raulston might lose the election.

On Monday, May 25, 1925, the grand jury convened to hear testimony concerning the charge that John T. Scopes had taught the theory of evolution to his students in Dayton Central High School on April 24. The plaintiff on the original charge had been changed from George Rappelyea to Walter White, county superintendent of schools (it seemed more fitting), and, after the testimony of a few of Scopes' students, and Judge Raulston's instructions, the grand jury needed only one hour to return an indictment against the teacher. Bail was set at five hundred dollars and paid by the Baltimore Sun, H.L. Mencken's employer. The trial was set for July 10.

The defense counsel met in New York on the first of July, and two days later shocked the people of Dayton by announcing that they had officially requested that the trial be moved to the federal district court in Nashville. The move would not only thwart Rappelyea's original intentions, but would also remove William Jennings Bryan from the prosecution. Federal Judge John Gore, however, refused the request.

Festive Preparations. Preparations for the trial increased rapidly, as the town braced itself for the eagerly awaited onslaught of spectators. A festive mood swept through the streets as the courthouse received a fresh coat of paint, bleachers were erected on the lawn for speakers and evangelists, a barbecue pit was dug nearby, Pullman cars were ordered for additional housing, buttons proclaiming "Your old man's a monkey" were distributed, and loudspeakers were attached to the outside of the courthouse to carry the sounds of the battle to those unable to get seats inside. Scopes wandered around the town, helping where he could, and discovered that he was treated more as a celebrity than a criminal, for without him the circus could not have come to Dayton.

On the seventh of July, three days before the trial was to begin, the whole town turned out to meet the train bearing the Great Commoner - William Jennings Bryan. That night, at a banquet held in his honor at the Aqua Hotel, Bryan found himself sitting across from the young man whom he had come to prosecute. The two men from Salem, Illinois, chatted much of the evening, as Bryan helped himself to the uneaten portion of Scopes' dinner.

On that same day Clarence Darrow quietly entered Dayton. As he walked down the streets of the town he stopped to talk with the people he met. That night a dinner was given in his honor and Darrow, in his typical country manner, played down his "big-city" life and spoke of his days as a small-town lawyer in Ohio. To show their appreciation, the townspeople of Dayton awarded him the honorary title of "Colonel."

Although Judge Raulston's gavel had not yet fallen, the Scopes trial had unofficially begun.

THE TRIAL

The tenth of July dawned hot and clear. The courtroom on the second floor of the freshly painted Rhea County Courtroom soon filled to its capacity as four hundred people occupied chairs and dozens more stood in available spaces. Townspeople, farmers, hill people, students, hawkers, evangelists and reporters jammed into the newly whitewashed room where the temperature would soon exceed one hundred degrees. A few minutes before the trial was set to open, Mrs. William Jennings Bryan was escorted up the aisle in her wheelchair to take what would become her customary place behind her husband's chair.

The members of the prosecution entered first and took their seats at the table facing the judge's bench. The local district attorney, Thomas Stewart, headed the prosecution and was accompanied by General Ben G. McKenzie, J. Gordon McKenzie (his son), Sue and Herbert Hicks, William Jennings Bryan, and William Jennings Bryan, Jr.

A few minutes later Clarence Darrow led the defense counsel and the defendant, John Thomas Scopes, to their table, which sat on the Judge's right, facing the jury box and with their backs to the wall. With Darrow and Scopes were John Randolph Neal, Arthur Garfield Hays, and Dudley Field Malone.

Judge John Tate Raulston then entered the already steaming courtroom. Before calling the court to order, though, Judge Raulston permitted the members of the press to take pictures of the prosecution, defense, and himself. The gavel dropped, and Judge Raulston called the Eighteenth Judicial Circuit Court to order. The Scopes Monkey Trial had begun.

Court Begins With Prayer. To the amazement of the defense lawyers from Chicago and New York, Judge Raulston immediately called upon the Reverend Cartwright to open the session with a prayer. Reverend Cartwright rose and, in a five-minute prayer, asked that God grant the court the wisdom to "transact the business of this court in such a way and manner as that Thy name may be honored and glorified among men." The rest of the day was spent selecting the jury and court was adjourned till Monday.

Bryan Speaks To Congregation. Over the weekend both sides spent a good deal of time in consultation and research, yet Darrow took time to present to the press some of the defense's arguments. On Sunday morning Bryan spoke before the congregation of the Southern Methodist Church with Judge Raulston and his family sitting in the first row. That afternoon Bryan addressed a huge crowd on the courthouse lawn. In his speech he welcomed the chance to bring "this slimy thing, evolution, out of the darkness…. Now," he said, "the facts of religion and evolution would meet at last in a duel to the death."

Monday, July 13

After a slight delay while technicians finished preparations for station WGN's broadcast live from the Rhea County courthouse, Judge Raulston called court to order and requested the Reverend

Moffett to open the second session with a prayer. It was soon evident that everyone was in for another day of courtroom temperatures near or above one hundred degrees and before the day was through every member of the prosecution and defense, save one, and Judge Raulston had removed their coats. Although several people passed out from the heat, Dudley Field Malone remained erect and dignified with his New York tailored double-breasted suit firmly buttoned.

John Randolph Neal of the defense rose and, in a long and tedious address, moved that the court quash the indictment against Scopes. Before Neal revealed the basis for the defense's move, Judge Raulston dismissed the jury from the courtroom while he listened to arguments. The remainder of the morning and most of the afternoon was a dull affair for the audience as Neal dryly contended that the Butler Act violated his defendant's freedom of speech and due process of law. Each lawyer, in turn (with the exception of Bryan), either defended or attacked the motion. Darrow closed the argument for the defense and gave the audience their first taste of what was to come.

After a casual, low-key opening that relaxed the audience and the jury, Darrow suddenly wheeled around and bitterly lashed out at Bryan. The move caught everyone, and especially Bryan, off-guard. His voice rising, Darrow attacked Bryan and the Fundamentalists for their attempt to force the public schools to conform their subject matter to the Bible:

The Bible is not one book. The Bible is made up of sixty-six books written over a period of about one thousand years, some of them very early and some of them comparatively late. It is a book primarily of religion and morals. It is not a book of science. Never was and was never meant to be.... They thought the

sun went around the earth and gave us light and gave us night. We know better. We know the earth turns on its axis to produce days and nights. They thought the earth was 4,004 years old before the Christian era. We know better.

Neither the audience nor the judge nor the jury had seen anything like the display Darrow exhibited that afternoon as he stormed and joked and gestured and laughed and fascinated everyone in the room. As the words began to sink into the minds of those packed into the second-story courtroom, they began to think and talk about evolution as they had never thought and talked before. Gradually they began to realize that evolution, as explained by Darrow, was not quite the same as that illustrated by their Fundamentalist preachers.

Before he could finish though, Judge Raulston interrupted to ask him to conclude his remarks the following day. Darrow disregarded the judge's request and finished his speech:

Ignorance and fanaticism is ever busy and needs feeding...today it is the public school teachers...after a while it is the setting of man against man and creed against creed until with flying banners and beating drums we are marching backward to the glorious ages of the sixteenth century when bigots lighted fagots to burn men who dared to bring any intelligence and enlightenment and culture to the human mind.

Tuesday, July 14

The courtroom was packed on Tuesday morning in anticipation of Judge Raulston's ruling on the defense motion to dismiss the indictment. Judge Raulston asked Reverend Stribling to open the third session with a prayer, but before he could do so, Darrow was on his feet with an objection. The move shocked the members of the audience, the prosecution, and Judge Raulston, for, as he explained, it had been his practice to open each session over which he presided with a prayer.

Darrow explained that in a case of this nature, wherein a conflict between science and religion forms the basis of the indictment, the opening of each session with a court-sanctioned prayer jeopardized his client's case. After brief arguments by both sides, Judge Raulston overruled Darrow's objection and Reverend Stribling proceeded to deliver his prayer.

Judge Raulston announced to the lawyers that due to a two-hour power failure on the previous night he had not yet reached a decision concerning the move to quash the indictment. After fifteen minutes of picture-taking, the judge adjourned court.

Wednesday, July 15

Judge Raulston read to the court (minus the jury again) his decision concerning the defense motion. Using the same arguments presented by District Attorney Stewart in opposing the motion, Judge Raulston overruled the motion and ordered that the trial proceed.

After the noon recess Judge Raulston asked the defense to enter their defendant's plea. Mr. Neal replied, "Not guilty." At that point Mr. Stewart briefly outlined the prosecution's case in a two-sentence statement to the defense.

In speaking for his colleagues Darrow, Neal, and Hays, Malone alleged that, according to the Butler Act, the prosecution had to prove that John T. Scopes made two distinct actions: first, that he "taught a theory that denies the story of the divine creation of man as taught in the Bible, and, second, that instead and in place of this theory he taught that man is descended from a lower form of animals." According to Malone, the defense would not argue the charge that Scopes did, indeed, violate the second part of the Butler Act when he taught his students Darwin's theory of evolution, but the defense would contest any statement on behalf of the prosecution that insinuated without proof that by teaching that man is descended from a lower form of animals Scopes automatically denied the story of creation as revealed in Genesis. If the court upheld the defense's "two-act" theory, then, according to Malone, "the prosecution must prove as part of its case what evolution is." He continued:

> **...we shall show by the testimony of men learned in science and theology that there are millions of people who believe in evolution and in the stories of creation as set forth in the Bible and who find no conflict between the two.**

In the eyes of the prosecution, the Butler Act forbade one act: teaching a theory that man is descended from a lower form of animals, for to them this action automatically denied the divine theory of creation according to the Bible. But the defense interpreted the Butler Act to forbid two actions: teaching a theory that man is descended from a lower form of animals, and denying the divine theory of creation according to the Bible. To prove the second part, Malone contended, scientific witnesses would have to be called to the stand to testify as to whether or not teaching Darwin's theory of evolution subsequently denied the divine theory of creation.

At the conclusion of Malone's presentation, Judge Raulston swore in the jury that had been selected five days earlier. At that point Attorney General Stewart called the prosecution's first witness, Superintendent of Schools Walter White, to verify that Scopes did indeed teach science in Dayton and that he had admitted in Robinson's Drug Store that he had taught evolution to his students. Darrow's cross-examination was brief, for he made no attempt to contest White's statements. Stewart then called to the stand Howard Morgan, a fourteen-year-old student of Scopes. Howard testified that Scopes had taught his class the theory of evolution, but Darrow brought out that Howard, like most students, remembered little of that day's lesson. The cross-examination of Howard Morgan and the next witness, Harry Shelton, was not as important to Scopes' case as was the manner in which Darrow talked to the boys.

Rather than with a serious, skeptical attitude, Darrow spoke to the boys as a friend would. He made light of the subject and kept the audience chuckling at his questions. There seemed to be no purpose in his line of questioning, but he deftly kept the audience from taking the testimony on evolution too seriously.

Attorney General Stewart then called upon F.E. Robinson, owner of Robinson's Drug Store and chairman of the board of education, to testify that Scopes had stated in his store that science teachers could not teach biology without discussing the theory of evolution. Darrow, in his cross-examination, read into the record the pages from Hunter's *Civic Biology* concerning the theory of evolution. The only point he attempted to emphasize was that Mr. Robinson, even though he was chairman of the school board, was the only person in Dayton who was authorized to sell the textbook which Scopes was arrested for teaching from. After Darrow finished, Stewart read into the record the first two chapters of Genesis, and rested the state's case.

Darrow opened the case for the defense by calling to the stand Dr. Maynard M. Metcalf, a former research professor in zoology at Johns Hopkins University and a Congregationalist deacon. Metcalf, like the eleven other scientists prepared to testify for the defense, was chosen not solely for the light he could shed on the theory of evolution, but also as an example of a scientist who was also a prominent church member. He represented the defense's first step in their attempt to prove that the theory of evolution does not necessarily contradict the Biblical theory of the divine creation.

Before Darrow had progressed very far with Metcalf, Steward interrupted to explain that as a matter of procedure, the defense had to call as their first witness the defendant (Scopes) or not call him at all. Darrow shrugged and prepared to continue with Metcalf. Judge Raulston, though, did not intend to treat the matter so lightly; he overruled normal procedure and gave Darrow the opportunity to call Scopes to the stand.

Darrow - Your honor, every single word that was said against this defendant, everything was true.

Raulston - So he does not care to go on the stand?

Darrow - No, what is the use?

As Metcalf prepared to explain the theory of evolution to the court, Stewart interrupted again, this time to object to the admission of scientific testimony into the trial. Raulston dismissed the jury again (much to their dissatisfaction), but agreed to hear Metcalf's testimony as an example of the type of testimony the defense planned to present before the jury. At the conclusion of Darrow's questioning, Judge Raulston ordered each side to prepare its arguments concerning the admission of expert testimony for the next day, and adjourned the court.

Thursday, July 16

The fifth day of the trial promised to be the most exciting yet. The question that was the key to the defense case was about to be discussed and answered: Could scientists be called as witnesses to define and explain the theory of evolution, and testify as to whether or not it necessarily conflicted with the Biblical account of the divine creation?

The morning was spent with prosecution and defense alternating arguments. Few people left their seats during the noon respite and those who did were quickly replaced, for the audience knew that the Great Commoner, William Jennings Bryan, would rise and speak that afternoon for the first time in the trial. Judge Raulston opened the afternoon session with a reminder to the audience of the great burden of weight that was being supported by the second-story floor and a suggestion that they **refrain** from any applause or outbursts.

After Darrow announced that Mr. Malone would be the last speaker for the defense, Judge Raulston motioned for Mr. Bryan to begin. The balding, sixty-five-year-old orator rose and approached the bench. Bryan defended and explained the one-act theory held by the defense and reviewed for the court the testimony of Mr. White and Mr. Robinson, who had testified that Scopes had admitted teaching evolution. "That is the evidence before this court, and we do not need any expert to tell us what that law means.... This is not the place to try to prove that the law ought never to have been passed."

As Bryan began warming to his subject, he began to captivate the minds and emotions of the jury and the audience. In turn he hit upon almost all of his favorite subjects: evolution, Prohibition, New York, majority rule, and when reason failed him, turned to humor to discredit the defense lawyers, Hunter's *Civic Biology*, and Charles Darwin.

In attempting to discredit the one scientist who had testified, Bryan vainly boasted that he had more degrees (yet all but one honorary) than did Professor Metcalf. After some verbal sparring with both Malone and Darrow, Bryan built towards his **climax**. He concluded his defense of the motion to exclude scientific testimony with:

> **The Bible is not going to be driven out of this court by experts who come hundreds of miles to testify that they can reconcile evolution, with its ancestor in the jungle, with man made by God in His image, and put here for purposes as part of the divine plan. No, we are not going to settle that question here, and I think we ought to confine ourselves to the law and to the evidence that can be admitted in accordance with the law.**

The applause was tumultuous and prolonged, and Judge Raulston made no attempt to stop it. Bryan calmly sat down and began to contemplate his victory over the defense, Darwin, and evolution.

After a short recess, Dudley Field Malone prepared to make the final defense plea against the motion. He rose and, with every pair of eyes in the courtroom on him, slowly and dramatically removed his coat for the first time in five scorching days. He folded it neatly and laid it across the table. The effect was astounding. It seemed as if everyone was holding his breath, not daring to make a move or emit a sound. Malone had deftly swept their attention from the echoes of Bryan's words without having said a word.

He opened his address slowly and deliberately, reflecting upon Bryan and what Bryan had said concerning Darwin and evolution.

> I have never seen harm in learning and understanding, in humility and open-mindedness, and I have never seen clearer the need of that learning than when I see the attitude of the prosecution, who attack and refuse to accept the information and intelligence which expert witnesses will give to them.

He returned, then, to the defense's two-act theory and, in reference to the passage in the Butler Act under interpretation ("...to teach any theory that denies the story of the divine creation of man as taught in the Bible, and to teach him that man is descended from a lower order of animals"), said:

> If that word had been "or" instead of "and," then the prosecution would only have to prove half of its case. But it must prove, according to our contention, that Scopes not only taught a theory that man had descended from a lower order of animal life, but at the same time, instead of that theory, he must teach the theory which denies the story of the divine creation set forth in the Bible. And we maintain

that we have a right to introduce evidence by these witnesses that the theory of the defendant is not in conflict with the theory of creation in the Bible.

Judge Raulston then asked Malone:

In other words, you believe...when the Bible says that God created man, you believe that God created the life cells and that then out of that one single life cell the God created man by a process of growth or development - is that your theory?

"Yes," said Malone and continued, his voice growing louder:

The least that this generation can do, your honor, is to give the next generation all the facts, all the available data, all the theories, all the information, that learning, that study, that observation has produced - give it to the children in the hope of heaven that they will make a better world of this than we have been able to make of it. We have just had a war with twenty million dead. Civilization is not so proud of the work of the adults. Civilization need not be so proud of what the grown-ups have done. For God's sake let the children have their minds kept open - close no doors to their knowledge; shut no door from them. Make the distinction between theology and science. Let them have both. Let them both be taught. Let them both live.

Malone then directed his attack on Bryan and his charge on Sunday that "the facts of religion and evolution would meet at last in a duel to the death." With a roar Malone turned to Bryan and concluded his feverish attack:

We are ready to tell the truth as we understand it and we
do not fear all the truth that they can present as facts. We
are ready. We are ready. We feel we stand with progress.
We feel we stand with science. We feel we stand with
intelligence. We feel we stand with fundamental freedom
in America. We are not afraid. Where is the fear? We
meet it. Where is the fear? We defy it. We ask your honor
to admit the evidence as a matter of correct law, as a
matter of sound procedure and as a matter of justice to
the defendant in this case.

Pandemonium broke loose. None of the previous applause could
compare with the wild cheering that followed Malone's speech.
Judge Raulston tried futilely to restore order. The cheering
lasted twice as long as it did less than an hour earlier when it
appeared that Bryan had secured the day for the prosecution.
It was reported that Darrow was concerned that Malone might
have convinced two of the jurymen to find Scopes innocent and
thwart their chance for an appeal in the Supreme Court. Malone
returned to the defense table where he was mobbed with
congratulations.

After order was finally restored, Stewart closed the argument
for the prosecution, but Malone's words were still in the minds
of the people packed in the courtroom and scattered in the
courtyard beneath the loudspeakers. As the courtroom emptied
minutes later, a stunned Bryan stopped by Malone's table and
said, "Dudley, that was the greatest speech I have ever heard."
Malone replied, "Thank you, Mr. Bryan. I am sorry it was I who
had to make it."

Friday, July 17

Although the defense had won the support of many with their attempt to bring the facts of evolution to light, Darrow realized that Raulston, in calmer repose, would probably rule against the admission of the scientists' testimony into the trial. Therefore, he instructed all of the scientists whom they had assembled in Dayton to prepare statements summarizing what, given the opportunity, they would have testified. When Raulston discovered the scientists dictating their statements to the court stenographer Friday morning, he ordered Darrow not to release them to the press, but Darrow curtly replied that the statements would, indeed, be released.

After court opened with the customary prayer and objection, Judge Raulston read to the court his decision to exclude expert testimony from the trial. He upheld the one-act theory of the prosecution and the constitutionality of the law. As far as he was concerned, the purpose of the trial was simply to decide whether or not John T. Scopes had taught the theory of evolution in a public school.

Raulston did, however, permit the defense to read into the record summaries of the statements made by the scientists for possible use in an appeal, and at 10:30 Judge Raulston adjourned court until Monday to allow the defense time to prepare their summaries.

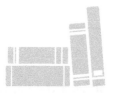

GLOSSARY

. . . .

Many of the words and phrases incorporated into *Inherit the Wind* by playwrights Lawrence and Lee to capture the flavor of the times were rather unique to early twentieth century America, the geographical location of the Scopes Trial, and the controversial conflict between science and religion. To aid the modern student in his/her understanding and appreciation of the work, these words, and others, are either defined or explained below:

Agnostic

One who believes that man is incapable of ever truly knowing whether or not God or any Ultimate Reality actually exists.

Alpaca

A fabric made from the hide of a South American animal similar to a llama.

Atheist

One who denies the existence of God.

Barnum and Bailey.

A famous traveling circus in America in the late 1800s.

Bible Belt.

Phrase coined by columnist H. L. Mencken to refer to the area in the South noted for its religious fundamentalism.

Blasphemies.

Irreverent words or actions against anything held sacred.

Caricature.

A picture, description, or portrayal in which the peculiarities or defects of a person or persons are exaggerated.

Charlemagne (742-814 A.D.).

Emperor of the Holy Roman Empire from 800 to 814.

Chautauqua.

An institution in the late 1800s and early 1900s that provided popular education for thousands of people through lectures and music, often held outdoors or in huge tents.

Coxey, Jacob (1854-1951).

A social reformer who led a group of unemployed and dissatisfied men to Washington, D.C. in 1894 to protest high unemployment; they were arrested on the Capitol lawn.

Dogma.

A system of principles or beliefs.

Dreyfus, Alfred (1859-1935).

A French military officer of Jewish descent who was convicted of treason in 1844 and 1899, but acquitted in 1906.

Effrontery.

Shameless boldness.

Elijah.

A Hebrew prophet in the ninth century before Christ.

Enunciator.

Microphone.

Fatuity.

Foolishness.

Firmament.

Heavens.

Flivver.

Small, cheap automobile.

Galluses.

Suspenders.

Happy Hooligan, Barney Google, Abe Kabibble.

Newspaper cartoon characters.

Hearsay.

Unofficial information gained from a second person rather than from the original source; gossip.

Heathen.

One who does not acknowledge the Christian God of the Bible; an irreligious person.

Henry's Lizzie.

A reference to Henry Ford and the small, cheap automobile his company produced from 1908 to 1927.

Heresies.

Opinions which differ with those of a standard church or religious system.

Heretic.

One who does not conform with an established attitude or doctrine.

Hinterland.

Remote or less developed area.

Houdini, Harry (1874-1926).

Famous magician and escape artist.

Hurdy-Gurdy.

A barrel organ played by turning a crank.

Infidel.

One who does not believe in Christianity.

Innocuously.

Harmlessly.

Irreconcilable.

Incapable of being brought into harmony.

Linotype.

Typesetting machine used in newspaper production.

Marconi, Guglielmo (1874-1937)

Inventor of the wireless telegraph.

Melange.

Mixture.

Monkeyshines.

Pranks.

Pagan.

Irreligious.

Pariah.

Outcast.

Pentateuch.

The first five books of the Hebrew Bible or the Old Testament.

Perdition.

Hell.

Petulant.

Irritated, annoyed.

Pith.

Sponge tissue.

Rotogravure.

Print or photograph.

Saint George.

Patron saint of England, who, according to legend, saved a young maiden from a dragon.

Socrates (470-399 B. C.).

Famous Greek philosopher.

Sodom and Gomorrah.

Ancient cities destroyed, according to the book of Genesis, as a result of their wickedness.

Sotto Voce.

Low, soft voice.

Unctuously.

In a smooth, suave, smug manner.

Venireman.

Person called for jury duty.

QUESTIONS FOR REVIEW

....

ACT ONE

Short Answer Questions

1. Why was Bert Cates arrested?

2. What major conflict does Rachel face in the first scene?

3. How does Mr. Meeker describe Matthew Harrison Brady?

4. What is Brady's chief vice?

5. Why is Henry Drummond associated with devil imagery?

6. What does Brady predict Drummond will do in court?

7. What is an agnostic?

8. What is Drummond's reason for coming to Hillsboro to defend Cates?

9. Why has Brady, according to Hornbeck, come to Hillsboro?

10. What two things does Drummond object to after the jury has been selected?

Discussion Questions

1. What is Cates trying to explain to Rachel when he says, "at the top of the world the twilight is six months long"?

2. Cite examples to show how the residents of Hillsboro view the approaching trial.

3. Why do people resist changing their traditions and abandoning their "old wives' tales"?

4. What is Drummond's philosophy of language?

5. Discuss Drummond's statement "The man who has everything figured out is probably a fool."

ACT TWO

Short Answer Questions

1. What does the Reverend Brown do that causes his followers to desert him and Brady to interrupt his prayer meeting?

2. According to Drummond, why have he and Brady moved so far apart?

3. How does Drummond gain supporters like Howard Blair?

4. Why did Cates leave the church?

5. What reason does the judge give for prohibiting scientific testimony?

6. What three persons from the Bible does Drummond question Brady about?

7. What does Henry Drummond consider holy?

8. According to the Bible, when did the creation begin?

9. What controversial question leads to Brady's downfall?

10. What weakness in Brady leads to his ridicule at the hands of Drummond?

Discussion Questions

1. What did Bert Cates probably mean when he supposedly said, "God created man in His own image - and man, being a gentleman, returned the compliment"?

2. How does the defense reconcile the theory of evolution and the Bible?

3. How does Drummond's speech on progress hold true today?

4. What roles do Right and Truth play in our lives?

5. Discuss how and why the attitude of the townspeople changes during the trial.

ACT THREE

Short Answer Questions

1. What is Brady doing as the act opens?

2. What does the radio symbolize?

3. What does the mayor tell the judge?

4. What error in procedure does the judge make?

5. Why does Brady react to the judge's fine?

6. What three things combine to lead to Brady's collapse?

7. What book helps prompt Rachel's decision to leave Hillsboro and her father?

8. Why does Drummond defend Brady against Hornbeck's's attack?

9. According to Hornbeck, what actually killed Brady?

10. What two books does Drummond slap together at the end of the play?

Discussion Questions

1. How do Lawrence and Lee justify Rachel's change in character?

2. How does Drummond's "Golden Dancer" speech relate to the play?

3. Discuss what Drummond meant when he said that "Brady got lost... because he was looking for God too high up and too far away."

4. What does Hornbeck mean when he calls Drummond "an atheist who believes in God"?

5. How does the quotation "He who troubleth his own house shall inherit the wind; and the fool shall be servant to the wise in heart" apply to the play and its characters?

ANSWERS TO SHORT ANSWER QUESTIONS

Act One

1. For teaching the theory of evolution to his sophomore class

2. The conflict between her feelings for her father and her love for Bert

3. Presidential candidate, loud, Chautauqua speaker

4. Food

5. To contrast him with Brady, who is considered the defender of the faith

6. Put the law on trial rather than the defendant

7. Someone who does not believe it can be proven that God does or does not exist

8. To prevent people like Brady from controlling the education of students, and to defend the freedom of speech

9. To "find himself a stump to shout from"

10. The prayer meeting announcement by the judge and the "Read Your Bible" sign

Act Two

1. Calls down a curse on Cates and Rachel

2. Because Brady has not progressed, he has been "standing still"

3. By being friendly, sincere, and by speaking in their own style of language

4. Over a disagreement with the Reverend Brown's handling of the funeral service of the boy who drowned

5. As not applying to the case at hand since the law is not on trial

6. Jonah, Joshua, Cain's wife.

7. "The individual human mind"

8. Around 4000 B.C.

9. That concerning the length of the first three days of creation

10. His vanity

Act Three

1. Eating

2. Progress

3. That the lawmakers in the state capital want him to "go easy" on Cates

4. Forgetting to give the defendant the right to make a statement prior to the sentence

5. Because he expected it to be more severe

6. The heat, overeating, and his frustration at his rejection by his followers

7. *Origin of Species*

8. Because he believes that even Brady had the right to think and to speak out

9. A "busted belly"

10. *Origin of Species* and the Bible

BIBLIOGRAPHY

LAWRENCE AND LEE

Lawrence, Jerome and Lee, Robert E. "The Genesis and Exodus of the Play." *Theatre Arts,* August 1957.

Lee, Robert E. "The Theatre of Optimism." *Cimarron Review,* June 1969, pp. 5-15.

THE SCOPES MONKEY TRIAL

Allen, Leslie H., ed. Bryan and Darrow at Dayton: The Record and Documents of the "Bible-Evolution Trial." *New York: A. Lee and Company, 1925.*

Grebstein, Sheldon Norman. *Monkey Trial: The State of Tennessee vs. John Thomas Scopes.* Boston: Houghton Mifflin, 1960.

Hays, Arthur Garfield. *Let Freedom Ring.* New York: Boni and Liveright, 1937.

____. "Strategy of the Scopes Defense." *Nation,* 5 August 1925, pp. 157-158.

Mencken, H.L. "In Tennessee." *Nation,* 1 July 1925, pp. 21-22.

____. "Editorial on Dayton." *American Mercury,* October 1925, p. 6.

Scopes, John T., and Presley, James. *Center of the Storm: Memoirs of John T. Scopes*. New York: Holt, Rinehart, and Winston, 1967.

CLARENCE DARROW

Darrow, Clarence. *Absurdities of the Bible*. Girard, Kansas: Haldeman-Julius Publications, 1931.

Haldeman-Julius, Marcet. *Clarence Darrow's Two Great Trials*. Girard, Kansas: Haldeman-Julius Publications, 1927.

Weinberg, Arthur, ed. *Attorney for the Damned*. New York: Simon and Schuster, 1957.

WILLIAM JENNINGS BRYAN AND FUNDAMENTALISM

Bryan: William Jennings, and Bryan, Mary Baird. *The Memoirs of William Jennings Bryan*. Chicago: John C. Winston Company, 1925.

Cole, Stewart G. *The History of Fundamentalism*. New York: Richard R. Smith, Inc., 1931.

Furniss, Norman F. *The Fundamentalist Controversy, 1918-1931*. New Haven, Connecticut: Yale University Press, 1954.

Levine, Lawrence W. *Defender of the Faith - William Jennings Bryan: The Last Decade, 1915-1925*. New York: Oxford University Press 1965.

H. L. MENCKEN

Manchester, William Raymond. *Disturber of the Peace: The Life of H. L. Mencken.* New York: Harper, 1951.

Mencken, H.L. The Days of H.L. Mencken: Happy Days, Newspaper Days, Heathen Days. *New York: Alfred A. Knopf, 1947.*

CHARLES DARWIN AND THE THEORY OF EVOLUTION

Darwin, Charles. *The Descent of Man and Selection in Relation to Sex.* New York: D. Appleton and Company, 1896.

____. *Origin of Species.* Edited by Morse Peckham. Philadelphia: University of Pennsylvania Press, 1959.

Hull, David L. *Darwin and His Critics.* Cambridge, Massachusetts: Harvard University Press, 1973.